Korea My Homeland

poems by

Han-Jae Lee

Finishing Line Press
Georgetown, Kentucky

Korea My Homeland

ACKNOWLEDGMENTS

The author would like to thank the editors of the following publications in which these poems have appeared, some in earlier versions:

Caesura: "Invisible Leash"
Crab Orchard Review: "Wasted Tire"
Catamaran Literary Reader: "Cobweb"
Monterey Poetry Review: "Flower Watch," "The Sorrow"
Sand Hill Review: "Secluded Life," "Times Square," "Pedestrian Crosswalk at Times Square"
PCC Inscape Magazine: "Heavy Rain Showers"
Military Experience & The Arts: "Outside the National Cemetery"
EMRYS Journal: "Magnolia"

Many thanks to the publisher and editors at Finishing Line Press for selecting this book for publication and for being so nice.

Special thanks to beloved my family and friends who gave me support and encouragement during the writing of this book.

And gratitude to all of my teachers and poets who helped me to shape these poems: Alexander E. Braun, Barbara Beswetherick, Judy Bernstein, Yvonne Cannon, Magdalena Montagne, Jennifer Franklin, Gillian Cumming, Kenneth Share, Aubrey Moncrieffe, Rosanne English, Gi-Taek Kim, Yeung-Nam Kim, Su-Ik Lee, and other too numerous to name.

Publisher: Leah Maines
Editor: Christen Kincaid
Cover Art: Mike Seungwook Lee
Author Photo: Mike Seungwook Lee
Cover Design: Leah Huete

Printed in the USA on acid-free paper.
Order online: www.finishinglinepress.com
also available on amazon.com

Author inquiries and mail orders:
Finishing Line Press
P. O. Box 1626
Georgetown, Kentucky 40324
U. S. A.

Table of Contents

III.

IV.

for my dear family

I.

Korea My Homeland

Korea! My native land!
Just hearing the name makes my heart flutter.

How long I have lived away from my native country!
Even though I can never forget it in my dreaming.

My homeland in the Far East.
This pleasant country where my ancestors dwelled for thousands of years.

A free county defended from the invasions of foreign nations.
In the ruins of war bloomed the rose of freedom.

Where the sun first comes up on the continent.
Where there are four seasons.

In March the countryside feels the start of spring.
My rural home with its rocks and hills.

The peaches and apricots in full bloom.
The breezes blowing soft and fresh.

Though time and tides flow away,
spring, summer, autumn and winter will return there
again and again.

Are my childhood friends still living there, I wonder?
Even though I am far away from my home
this yearning makes me grow fonder.

Loving this land where cherished dreams are realized.
I would like to mount up to the sky like a huge white crane
and see Korea again.

San Francisco

My friend, you will see the seashore
where the splendid blue sky
pours down its pails of glaring sunlight;
nearby ridges beckoning to come
on wings of fresh green foliage.

Where often chilly wind
wafts in from the Pacific;
this is San Francisco.

When you come here, my friend
you will find the Golden Gate Bridge
the pink of cherry blossoms
connecting north and south.

We could lounge on Baker Beach.
And at Fisherman's Wharf we could cook the entire coastline!
At the Gold Dust Lounge we'll drink and dance.

We could place our chairs facing the waves on the beach
and see a myriad of stars in the brilliant night sky
as we raise our eyes heavenward.

The fatigue of a long journey of flowing life behind us
we see a crowd,
a host of yellow daffodils,
fluttering and dancing alongside the beach
like the women we might meet.

Another World

I talked about the past with people I did not know
who looked like they came from dreams.

Their faces seemed picturesque
like the surface of meandering streams.
Their voices were a gentle breeze.

We walked along the village road—
the wildflowers in full bloom,
downy clouds dotting the sky.

Then, like an illusion
these strangers passed through the flowers
one by one.

I stopped walking and took a closer look at the flowers
comprised entirely of diverse unknowns.
Each one having its own life and universe.

After all the people were gone
I could only see myself.
A man who stood behind me.

Wet Fog

Wet fog comes frequently to Daly City.
Looks like fog the fine trees seem to murmur.
Wet fog blows up from the coast side of the Pacific.

Like the huge white cranes
whose wings spread throughout the city and one after another
suck up the parks, houses, streets, and people.

Wet fog doesn't talk all day long
and when the sunlight breaks through
returns to a far-off shore.

During its stay in the city
wet fog doesn't hurt even a petal or a dog.
Wet fog walks softly, laughing without sound, smiling…

Wishing to make friends with people
wet fog drops inside houses,
participates in parties and disappears.

When wet fog feels ennui it rises quickly and becomes the ridges of waves.
When it wishes to hear the sound of water
wet fog becomes the drizzling rain.

By the Golden Gate Bridge

After the fog lifts—a beautiful morning calm.
The broad sun comes up as usual.

The gentleness of heaven is on this bridge.
A massive structure of pink.

The bridge appears magnificent.
Wearing the beauty of the morning silently.
The blue sky overhead, bright and glittering.

Many visitors pass over the bridge
from many countries.
Whole generations.

The travel guide for San Francisco claims:
The earth hasn't anything to show more stately and beautiful
than the Golden Gate Bridge.

Perhaps it is this brilliance that causes
the impulse to jump into the waters below.

The loveliness of the bridge tarnished
by sadness and solemnity.

Above the blue and windy sea
the sun shines on the bridge.

On the Muni Bus in San Francisco

Rush hour is always crowded on the Metro.
More passengers are standing than sitting—
not even comprehending this inconvenience.

Along the route an electric signal
continuously informs travelers of the next stop
and the next.

On Monday mornings some people doze.
Someone gurgles with a cold.
A teenage boy, wearing headphones, laughs, while watching his mobile phone.

It seems the passengers have deep monologues inwardly.
But no one converses with each other.
Only an awkward silence hangs over them.

Perhaps they understand—
like a drunkard, or a farmer, returning to his grass hut in the late afternoon—
that to live is to keep silent.

At intervals, an elderly grandmother
coughs with a choking sound.
The passengers avert their eyes, closing them, or looking out the window.

Even when a disabled old man boards in a wheelchair
they stand aside for him
in silence.

While the Muni bus carries this tough life slowly
I recall nostalgic moments of bygone days
and hurl a handful of tears at the window.

In moments of reverie, I miss my stop.
Firmly grasping the call line to get off.

At the Subway

At the Powell station of the BART
in San Francisco
I see a foreigner carrying a heavy bag.

He asks me the way,
pointing to the subway map with his finger.
He seems to know no English.

When he speaks with embarrassment, I can't understand.
It looks like he is pointing to the symbol for the airport.
I can tell by his body language that he worries that he will miss his plane.

Suddenly I recall the days
when I didn't know my way on the subway
and puzzled over what to do.

It was not easy to explain to him
with gestures and movements
that the airport train would be arriving at the station shortly.

I watched him
as he tried to catch the train that was going the wrong way.
Knowing he was not going to get on the airport train.

His harried actions only made things more difficult for him.
His fingers moved faster as he talked to another stranger.
Groans came out of his mouth unconsciously.

There was no one to restrain his actions;
and not only the hour of the airplane's departure
seemed to be accelerating.

Spring Days' Rebellion

After frequently exchanging whispers
among the haze, breeze and sunshine of spring
this upheaval begins without notice.

At first this rebellion seems to be insignificant
but the days go by, the signs come from here and there,
and the weeds quickly spread through gardens, fields and streams.

Pushing the hard surface of the earth
the fresh green sprouts ascend from the soil;
there is no Maginot Line against them.

Yesterday's roads cast off their skin
and stirring from sleep the withering branches wriggle.
Rutting bamboo buds jump up from their roots.

The rebellion is pleasant all around
and the cheerful uprising is continued
until the coming brilliance of summer.

Although the woods suffered last winter,
the fallen leaves here and there joyfully sing for the coming days;
forsythias open their eyes to see the green fields.

The aching remembrance of past seasons is not forgotten.
But the fragrance of the flowers tempt the bees to go out into the fields
and the tender smile of the southern breeze beckons

Welcome Spring

You, my lover of spring, who has returned to me.
Please give me the chance to embrace you again.
For I am penitent after my foolishness.

Yearning like an orphan who has lost his parents.
Hugging my heart.
My lover of spring.

Please help me recover the burning passion
that has cooled in your absence.
Let your warm smile sprout blossoms that have withered away.

You, my lover of spring,
I never groaned or complained of any discomfort
while I waited for you.

Let's enjoy a picnic under the cherry blossoms.
Let's sing in chorus.
Welcome spring!

You, my lover of spring, who has come back again.
Let's go together and not separate again.

Whispers of Spring

I open the window suddenly,
believing I hear
last year's fallen leaves
rustling in the wind.
But they are not there.

Instead, I hear whispers
from the yellow sprouts
of forsythia in the garden.
Buds just forming
from thin branches.
Perhaps the yellow color of buds
call and halt me.

In the park—branches of white magnolias in full bloom,
red azaleas and pink cherry blossoms
moving in the breeze.
Their flowers come early,
before their leaves.

Messengers of the season, they knock.
First to awaken spring!
Bringing the light of the sun.
Causing the streams to flow.
Singing a song that twittering birds join.
Forcefully launching a fresh spring.

These messengers tell me that spring has come.
But will vanish without much notice.

Cherry Blossoms

During the cherry blossom festival
pale pink flowers cover the entire sky.

Laughing and waving their hands
they gladly greet me.

Their sunny smiles and fresh smells
wash away the fatigue of daily life.

It's like a beauty contest
with musical instruments in a schoolgirls' band.

The flowers are singing songs all along
and even dancing in the breeze.

With all the flowers so similar
how do I choose the most beautiful?

Looking more closely, I see that, like the faces of people,
the countenances of the flowers are different.

Similarly, we may be seen as the same person by the flowers.
They have their own universe; embrace sunshine, dew, wind and sky
as they blossom uniquely.

How long will the festival of ecstasy continue?
Can they know the way to eternal joy?

Desires toward what is beautiful
may lead us endlessly.

Toward the End of Cherry Picking Season

Monday morning
after a weekend full of pickers.
Toward the end of cherry picking season.

All the lovely guests had come together
like the inflow of tides.

Taking joyfully the fresh and virgin cherries.
Until fully satisfied.

Now gone as tide ebbs.
Only a few cherries
hang lonely on the trees.

In order to be loved
the cherries waited a long time.
Together with the farmer from the beginning of spring.

The sky darkened with clouds and
peals of thunder were heard frequently.
The cherries brightened their bodies
with deep red lipstick.

The harmony of the cherries' colors and their dreams
at last fulfilled
by those who picked them.

Watermelon

She relaxes with a smile.
In joy and sorrow she welcomes all people
with looks of delight.

Her disposition is that of a good-natured person.
Though her external features have well-rounded corners
her heart is filled with sharp passions.

Her nature is to help others.
She gives willingly of herself
to those who are thirsty.

Reminds them not to swallow
the seeds,
while taking her flesh.

Morning Glory

Turning the corner in front of my house
a purple morning glory seems to beckon.
But I can't stop for her
or I'll be late for work again.

Even though I can see through the gaps in the fence
that she is blooming brightly
in the morning sunlight and dewy grasses
I cannot stop now.

She looks unwilling though to have me take leave.
Even bows down to me in the breeze.
I thought I would have time to love her
when I returned later.

However, she did not wait for me.

Though she had looked so gorgeous earlier
by the time I went back
in late afternoon
she had faded.

Dandelion

One yellow dandelion blooms
alone by the fence.
On the other side
people are busy coming and going.

The dandelion flower seems to have much curiosity about these people
and tries to lean toward the pedestrians.

But the dandelion leaf worries that someone will tread on the flower.
The leaf makes an effort to hold the petals back, so they do not lean.

The fence also exerts pressure on the flower—
holding her back.

The breeze blows over in the leaf's direction
trying to help the leaf stall the dandelion's progress.

Spring noon's sunshine falls in snatches around the pedestrians
creating power for the leaf through photosynthesis.

The dandelion, smaller than the other flowers,
is perhaps curious about tall things.

Eventually this curiosity turned into spores and dispersed in the air.
Then white dandelion seeds wandered away.

Riding the wind
flying fast to the end of the sky.

Cobweb

A spider, all alone, is building a cobweb in the corner of the hamlet.
His house waves in the breeze, shaded by a drift of clouds.

Though it is only sounds and sunshine that he hauls up,
he mends the net strand by strand, as if according to musical notation.

Which line has to be installed first or last? How long?
He is a skilled carpenter, humming to himself as he builds.

"What stays where the winds have passed?"
"How long will I have to wait?

Though it is only a shadow in the moonlight and on the morning dew,
he is never giving up on his house.

He continues to inhabit the garden
where the sparrows twitter and the children chatter.

The spider is conceiving a dream of a loving nest
within the cosmos that hugs the sky, villages and byways.

Cradle Song

Chirr! Chi—rr! Chirr! Chi—rr!
The cicadas sing again in my backyard, signaling the summer season.
A refrain that happens each night and day.

The song begins with a single cicada
but soon a number of insects are chirring together.
Lazily they sing, without doing any work like the industrious bees.

Listening long enough I hear a pattern in the chirring
and I try to view their chirrs as a delightful chorus of rural life.
But I hear the sound differently according to my mood.

When I feel comfortable after a meal, the intonation is a cradle song.
But after a day filled with annoyances, it becomes a bothersome noise
like the sound of someone weeping.

Evening Primrose

In summertime, the evening primrose
opens her yellow flowers
when the sun retires.

Because of loving the stars
she opens anew her exquisite blossoms
when night falls.

Because of loving the moon
the primrose blossoms alone
contrary to most of the other flowers
blooming only in daylight hours.

When the crescent moon appears
the primrose tells whimsical stories until dawn.
When the moon is full
she delights in animated conversation.

When there is no moon
she converses with the myriad stars and galaxies
in the brilliant night sky
about the mythologies of the constellations.

Lilacs Bloom Again

Lilacs bloom again.
Lilacs bloom again.
Light purple lilacs bloom again
by the grave of my love.

Spring has come again.
Spring breezes have blown in again.

Once I thought that the memory of our first kiss
under the lilac bush in the evening
and the solemn vow
like golden flowers
would vanish like a breeze
and be gone completely.

I made every effort to erase these memories, but in vain.
Now lilacs awaken within me the forgotten faint fragrance
and her warm breath.
Her bright smile
revealed by the lilac.

At first I hated these lilacs.
Forgotten love,
Unforgettable love.
She comes with the lilacs and vanishes silently.

Alas! I would never send her away.
And I call her name repeatedly.
Only my sorrow and sighing echoes into air.
Lilacs bloom again.

Magnolia

Just when I am getting into my car
someone seems to call to me.
I look back hastily.

I see my mother wearing white clothes
and smiling brightly
beyond the gate of the cemetery.

I return to her
as she waves both hands emphatically
crying out to me:

"Oh no, no, you are too late to come back to your home,
and you should not drive too fast on this road."

When I look again where she last stood
the magnolia tree with its white blossoms
is swaying in the breeze.

Apple Memories

At Hillview Farm each fall
apples hang in clusters
on the branches appetizingly.

I pick the ripe red apples,
filling basket after basket.
My children looking on.

More than the red fruit in my hands
these apples are made up of blue skies, water and wind
and pleasing sunshine.

After awhile the cheeks of the apples
look like the glowing cheeks
of my smiling children—
laughing happily
gathering up the fruit
scooping them into baskets.

And the apples also
seem to be laughing.

Do the apples keep these memories for a long time, I wonder?
Cherishing the fragrant air, released willingly,
selflessly shared year after year.

Do the apples treasure
the bright smiles of my children,
happily as their own?

April

April's cold claws still remain in places
and the winds in the alley
still blow harshly.

On the sunny side of the street a cat yawns.
Grinning from ear to ear it stretches out its front paws.
His protruding tongue lengthens to bathe its body, even its tail.
The helpful breeze licks, smooths down its fur.

The forsythia blooms its diminutive yellow petals.
A broody hen broods over her chicks.
One curious hatchling tries to climb onto its mother's back
slips down again and again.

Tree boughs stretch their bodies.
Their branches saturated by the spring haze.
Breezes extend their height long into the sky.

Coaxing the Buds into Flower

On my wife's birthday I bought her a bouquet
pink flowers in a white porcelain vase—
five lilies, five tulips, five roses.
Only the five lilies were not yet flowering.

But I was hopeful
the buds would burst
into blossom soon.

Each day I changed the water in the vase
and trimmed the bottom stems a little
to coax them into flowering.

Although the buds seemed to observe my efforts
they didn't open their petals easily.
And even after a week there was no sign of change.

By the time the blossoms of the tulips and the roses were falling from their stems
the petals of the lilies' budding flowers were only partially open.
Until one day I noticed their gaping mouths and the six petals formed fully.

Horizontal Line

Nobody can erase the vestige
of the sorrow of parting.

Though it may be embraced
by those who know this pain.

The traces of separation from earth and sky
and between them the evening glow of blood red tears
spread over a horizontal line.

Our meeting was not by chance, but by destiny.
So that we combined into one line horizontally
and our heart, you and I, we are one.

Sunrise and sunset on the line.
We share the pleasure and pain of life together.

Into the Clouds

I entrust my burdensome packages to airport staff.
Submit my weary self to an officer who inspects my body.
And after these bothersome procedures
I fly in an airplane with an empty feeling.

Banks of clouds build up along the western horizon.
We pass small cities just below us.
A river is moving away.
Mountains are receding altogether with long tails.

Like a balloon broken from its string
the plane goes up into the clouds.
I'm shown all kinds of palaces through my window—
villages, houses, animals...

The clouds are like magicians who build the world
without any troublesome measures.
Clouds demonstrate that to live is like the arising of clouds
and dying is like their disappearance.

Heavy Rain Showers

After the sweltering heat
that continued for two weeks
rain suddenly pours down.
For more than an hour it continues.

While low clouds hang ominously over the mountains
dark clouds rush in across the horizon.
And then the downtown is filled with deafening thunder—Kaboom!
It grows louder, hour by hour.

A short distance away the towering buildings
grow dim and invisible.
It is dark even in the afternoon.

The cries of birds cease.
They remain at their nesting places
aware of their surroundings.

During storms like these
I also feel the need to cower;
to take a backward glance at what I have been.

To Become One with Rain

First raindrops start to fall with a slow drip-drop...
But this quickly turns into a bigger sound—
pitter-patter, pitter-patter.
Then the flashes of lightning come together
with a mighty bang of thunder.

Crack! Rumble!
Rumble! Crack!
It rains.

Finally, summer showers!
After the hot and muggy weather of the weeks before—
when the air was like the inside of an oven—
it's a welcome relief
when the rain comes down.

Now, lightning flashes
and thunder fills the air.
The sky darkens.

Suddenly, I feel an impulse to run out into the downpour—
to ascend at full speed into the sky.
To become one with the rainstorm completely.

Whenever the thunder rolls, rain streaks the windows heavily.
And at this very moment
light and darkness have exchanged places.

Story of the Half Moon

In the garden my three-year-old son gestures toward the half moon.
"Where did the other half go?" "Why is it broken?" he asks me.

I remember now that he has seen a full moon only one time.
And I tell him that the other half of the moon is resting somewhere in heaven.

Now, when I look at the half moon, I imagine
the place she rests is somewhere I too could have a relaxing hiatus.

A place where I could restore my soul,
forgetting every inextricably bound thing of this world.

The Fountain

At a Mediterranean-blue lake in Las Vegas
fountains execute an aquatic ballet
choreographed to music and lights.

Water spouts rise up together, toward space;
swinging right and left with the melody
flexibly forming circles, parabolas, cylindrical bottles.

Some streams play a match—
Shooting upwards continually.
Attempting to reach sky upright.

But in a moment they understand.
There is no support for them on top.
Then they come back home to emptiness.

Sometimes the fountains spray over the air,
creating a misty lake and rainbows.
Night falls, and the colors are illuminated.
Spouts and lights cross over each other with wild abandon.

At midnight the performance stops suddenly.
Music and lights completely covered in darkness.

First Birthday

To an infant's bright smiles
we are playing the clown.
Laughing loud and long
at her first birthday party.

The infant keeps on laughing
as we set light to the candles.
We sing birthday songs in celebration
of this first birthday together.

Mortal life and bliss—
She doesn't know, nor does she care,
but creates pretty joy each day.
Opens blossoms, makes flowers.

Merry, merry baby!
What shall we call you?
Happiness and hope we call you.

The green field sleeps in the sun.
The small birds twitter.
The stream is flowing.

Cheerful you are, magnificent you are.
Let us keep your innocent smile long in our heart.
Think of us, lovely baby!

Can we cease to love you
when the candles are extinguished?

No, no! Surely we are with you always.
Until the end of our lives.
We love you forever!

Retired Men's Picnic

Picnic tables on an autumn afternoon in the village park.
Country friends have gathered for a barbecue cookout.

Each has his role.
One splits the wood for kindling,
another fans the fire; roasting beef on the broiler.
Another carries the meal to the table.

A drinking bout goes on simultaneously.
Some imbibe straight whiskey,
while others drink beer from bottles and cans.

With each drink
their voices grow louder.

They chain-smoke.
Revile their old bosses.
Cast aspersions on the president.

One complains about annuity insurance.
Compared to his payment
his pension is too small to live on,
his medical fees too expensive.

They repeat themselves endlessly.
There is no one to hear them.

Only the liquor bottles
look up at them
from the corners of their open mouths.

As the afternoon progresses
their tone sinks slowly
into tiredness.

Little by little
the wrinkled faces
are buried
in twilight.

Renaissance Woman

The *Seoul Supermarket* is always crowded.
The owner, Mrs. Kim greets customers with a "Hi."
Shaking hands and all the time smiling a toothy smile.

People prefer to call the market *Hi Super.*

Mrs. Kim is known as a renaissance woman.
Especially knowledgeable about the customs of Asian countries
and daily life in America. Mrs. Kim speaks fluent English.

Her husband, John, also greets every customer with "Hi."
They impart a generosity to Asian, European and African-Americans alike.
They do not forget to create a feast for them.
The customers are like close friends of the Kim's.

Yet, when friends ask to celebrate the Kim's wedding anniversary,
Mrs. Kim doesn't even know the date or the year of the marriage.

Dimple

Mary was my neighbor twenty years ago,
then left for New York City.
After that I forgot her.

By chance I met her at the shopping mall.
But when she called to me I didn't recognize her.
Her face was that of a common middle-aged lady.

At first I didn't answer.

Then she called me again, "Brother!
You are the same, like a young man."
And a smile spread across her face.

Then unexpectedly,
another Mary came out
from behind the aged lady's face.
Then I remembered her dimples when she smiled.

Her two high school daughters, taller than she
broke into a chorus of dimpled laughter.
Which, until this time, they had kept,
like a flower, all to themselves.

I Am Flying

I am flying in a plane over the Pacific; it is midnight.
I sleep in a lounge chair facing upward.
My first time flying business class.
The seat is as comfortable as the billowing clouds outside the window.

Up until now I sat in the narrow seats of economy class
unable to recline fully.
The front of the plane, first class,
is a place I had never experienced.

Before I had no interest in the classes of a plane.
Going by air was enough for me;
I never thought of comparing classes.
The idea of sitting in business class was someone else's story.
And I didn't care about other people's comfortable circumstances.

There are so many passengers in the back rows of the plane.
Before, I didn't feel the inconvenience of the constricted seats.
I feel compassion for them now,
as they sleep
curled up in their narrow seats.

We are all passengers in the same outer space.
Located at around thirty thousand feet.
Our departure time and destination the same.
Flying time will be around eleven hours,
but we are segregated by classes of seats.

Before, I could perceive the comfort of business class.
But when I imagined the first class seats
my business class seat also seemed insufficient.
In order to enjoy the comfortable life, perhaps,
we must look back into the past life of poverty.

At the Adult School

Isabella, a working mom with two jobs,
repeats the words in English
she is trying to memorize.

Before her eyes they seem to escape.
As soon as a word enters her right ear
it vanishes from her left.

Before she completes a page in her textbook
she forgets the contents of the first line.
Her second daughter's crying face appears in her memory.
The daughter who has caught a cold, again.

Isabella works at the laundry, part-time weekday afternoons;
at a fine restaurant in the evenings.
But she is dreaming of becoming a police officer.

Her classmate Daniel is an auto mechanic.
He is looking for words
in the dictionary
while listening to the teacher's lecture.

An old man who is retired writes words on a page.
He'd like to write his memoir in English.

Fifty students, whose motherland and races are different,
share their enthusiasm for revealing that their difficulties are the same.

Dozing

I wake to the sound of a waterfall—
a cruise over invisible Buffalo Falls;
I hear a burst of applause.

I notice a pool of saliva on my tan jacket;
Wipe it up.
Try not to doze off again.

To chase off my drowsiness
I hit my thigh, clear my throat, rub my eyes;
Certainly not! I will not fall asleep again!

I admonish myself.
Tilt my head to concentrate.
Absorb the lecture on philosophy.

After awhile I wake
to the noise of a crashing waterfall again.
But there is no water.

Only the din of applause
in the full conference room.

I ask myself: *Isn't this strange?*
I've never napped before
while listening to a teacher's lecture.

In this somnolent condition
I see myself now, trying to awaken.
But all self-persuasion is in vain.

As soon as I let myself off the hook
I plunge into Buffalo Falls again.
Startled by laughter as I shout for help.

Mountain in the Foreground

The mountain in the foreground of my village forecasts the weather.
In the morning I see the mountain's features from my bed.
Sunny days are a short distance away.

Sometimes dark clouds move across the mountain,
linger for a while on the ridge, then disappear
suddenly.

On other days gigantic cumulus clouds
hang on its peak—
a huge balloon.

In rainy season the mountain is covered with clouds, the mountain invisible for days.
Heavy clouds rush across the ridgeline,
then showers follow.

Sometimes the fog covers the forest,
spreads her skirt
all the way to the village.

In the evening the sky over the mountain
shows a halo round the moon.
And then I forecast it will rain tomorrow.

The mountain changes his clothes every season.
Sometimes it is green;
After that the hills are aflame with autumnal hues.
Even when I do not notice.

The mountain ridge is the gate of the sun, the moon and the birds.
Flocks of swans fly away just before sunset—
Orange in a sky full of purple feathers.
Before the winter snowcaps appear on top of the hill.

II.

Highway 5

I am driving from San Diego to San Francisco.
It is midnight.
In the rearview mirror of my minivan,
trucks, wagons and sedans pass me.

A limousine with opened windows
pulls up beside me.
The driver yawns heavily.
In a pink sleeveless dress a woman leans
on the arm of a man driving a convertible.

My speedometer reads seventy-five miles an hour.
I've already gulped three glasses of iced coffee,
but still feel drowsy.
Turned up the MP3 player.
Sung a song loudly.

I stretch my lower jaw right and left with a yawn.
The GPS reveals
the distance and time
left to travel.
I pinch the flesh of my thigh.
But it is all the same, sleepy.

In a few hours I will arrive home.
If I get over this moment.
But it is not easy.

This trip is hard like the stern realities of my life.
Troubles must be passed through.
Nobody can drive my life for me.
I will plow my way along the road.

If I get over this moment
the darkness will certainly be over.
The sun will shine brilliantly.

My heart is in my home, not here on the highway.
My heart lives for the coming day.
When there is an end to passing troubles.
And delight returns.

Surfing

I am surfing today, in the middle of the boundless Pacific.
Surfing on the rough waves.
Though I am exposed to rain and wind everyday
I continue surfing.

Even if great waves the size of mountains arise,
I will not stop,
nor stumble,
but only manage them
to move forward.

Sometimes the waves are calm.
But at any time without notice
a huge waves tackles me,
causes me to keel over
into deep water.

Waves are my close friends,
neighbors, my life's companions;
I cannot live without them.

Sea conditions may vary from time to time,
but in order to survive life's harsh passages
I choose waves that aren't too big or too little.

I am surfing today.
I am going through the rough waves
alone.

Leave It as It Is

I see her from across the channel liner,
a nameless, uninhabited, lush island
at the bosom of the Pacific
between San Francisco and Los Angeles.

Like an inquisitive child
she is on intimate terms with nature.

The birds begin to sing before the sun rises.
Those echoes resound
and the crystal streams glide
through the valley.

Buds come into bloom.
The merry birds sing a joyous song
while the young lambs bound
under leaves so green.

What beautiful scenery there is!

Breezes pass through the leaves.
She wants to sleep by the murmuring stream.
Disturb not her dream.

Pass through her land without stopping.
Flow gently to the seashore.
Don't drop your anchor to come up.
Don't pitch a tent, don't dig a well.
Flow gently along with the shore.

Her heart leaps up when she sees
a rainbow in the sky.
She is singing a song, the winds are breathing low
and the stars are burning bright.

Flow gently by, disturb not her land.
Leave her as she is.
Leave it as it is.

New York City

The city of all cities!
The city where people from every country live together.

At the United Nations' headquarters
you will be welcomed by the flags of all nations
flapping in the sparkling sunshine.
The flag of your homeland inspiring proud memories.

All the busy people!
Even so, when we struggle to find our way,
they help us kindly.
They do not lose their laughter.

When the stress of daily life accumulates
they go to Times Square
to sing and dance with friends.
Or take a break alone in midtown's Central Park.

When frustrating days greet you
look to the Statue of Liberty—icon of freedom.
She might give you wings
to fly to endless blue sky.

Thus and so, a beautiful night descends.
Numberless stars alight over the city.
Each room in the high-rise apartments is full of stories.
New Yorkers everywhere, like lovers that talk all night,
and awaken to conceive a happy dream the next morning.

The Umbrella

Autumn in New York's Central Park.
Rain again.

The fallen leaves once yellow, now brownish in color.
Scattered by the steps of visitors.

Autumn rains press the leaves to fall.

An old man sees a young couple
walking in front of him
under a partially torn
black umbrella.

The young man
holds the umbrella with one hand.
With the other
he hugs the young woman
at her waist.

Her arms entwined around his.
They are completely together.

Even though they are under the umbrella
they are soaked by the rain:
their shoulders, trousers, shoes.
Even though, they walk along humming.
Sometimes bursting into laughter.

The harder it rains
the closer they hug.
The umbrella binds them together.
A small and torn umbrella is joy enough.

Some Salesmen

David returns to Wall Street
where he and Michel sold
clothes and shoes.

They were poor and happy together then.
Driving their old Volkswagen Bus,
selling goods at a loss and at clearance.

Sometimes in the evenings they drank beer.
Disputed capitalism and business etiquette
all night long.

Once they opened a very small store
on the corner
of a back street.

Though they did their best
day and night to survive,
they finally closed it down.

Left with debt,
they scattered
each on their own.

The survival game too cold.

Now David stands in front of the banks at noon.
The buildings more magnificent and splendid than before.
There are many bankers in formal attire;
their faces beaming with smiles.

The small stores on the back streets are still shabby.
Many confusing signs have appeared,
but few people to read them.
Salesmen solicit them with no concern.

On the other side of the main street
hundreds of people are marching.
Demonstrating with the placard "Occupy Wall Street."
Shouting the slogan "We are the ninety-nine percent!" over and over.

But their slogan only scatters into the air.

Statue of Liberty

Legendary heroine, our pride.
Prophetess who wakes up the people.
Guardian deity of America.

In silence she asks those who are weary and oppressed to follow.
To look at the torchlight in her right hand,
hold a dream for the future,
keep on moving toward tomorrow.

Her exclamation echoes in our hearts and minds:
Through the Freedom Tower New York,
over oceans, throughout the world.

She is a mute pioneer.
There are no words that come from her.
But her grand silent gesture
is more eloquent than speech.

Ground Zero Memorial

In the memorial pools
the gentle melody of waves
softly resounding.

Victims' names etched on the surrounding panels
seem to go down with the waves.
Hand in hand in a gentle rhythm.

Waves cascade into a hole in the middle
together with noise and dust
hatred and earthly thoughts…

While the black hole before us in the center of the pool
absorbs all things—even the light—
the waves continue and continue.

It seems that through the waves
all things in nature are refined
and settle into another harmonic universe.

Perhaps visitors understand—like pilgrims to other sacred places—
that what is seen is temporary, what is unseen is eternal.
That to love is to keep an eon of silence hanging over them.

A Writing Class by the Railroad

Our classroom resembles a rural hut in the countryside.
In a renovated railroad station on the Hudson Valley.
The seasons seem to arrive earlier here.

At the writers' center students cultivate their creativity.
Exchanging opinions like farmers in this valley—
trading seeds, talking over the weather.
Their discussions continue until evening.

The sound of the railroad sparks their imagination.
The whistle so loud they cannot speak, but only look to each other.
Their hopes spreading out further, following the endless railroad.
Propelling them to fly upward toward blue skies, like the birds of this valley.

At the writing class on the Hudson River where the yachts anchor,
students primp their feathers like showy canvases to sail.
They are a step ahead of the seasons,
their enthusiasm leading the way.

Despite the noise of the train
the roses bloom beautifully
and the red apples are ripe on the trees.

Outside the National Cemetery

White magnolias brightly bloom
in the isolated places outside the national cemetery.

The white gravestones lined up in the cemetery
welcome the magnolias that come each year in April.

Wearing their white uniforms, the magnolias are like officers in the navy
receiving an inspection from their admiral.

The captivated white petals console the souls in the cemetery.
The souls of those who laid down their lives for their nation.

The souls beneath the gravestones have eagerly waited a long time
for their friends and relatives.

The magnolias ghostwrite the letters for the souls in their petals
and send them on the breeze to those who live in remote parts of the country.

On windy days they sing the song of April and dance with the branches
scattering the petals on the graves.

In the night sky interspersed with stars
the souls and petals are dreaming a dream together.

At the Unknown Soldiers' Monument

An invisible banner.
Unheard cry.
Of legendary heroes.
Obscure names.

We forgot you like a lost memory.
Enjoyed life with drinking and song
until hearing a trumpeter's requiem
on Memorial Day...

We look at the bundled flowers
before the spirits of the departed.
We pray and confess our stupidity.

You sink into oblivion while we consume ourselves.
Flinging our bodies into the sea of humanity,
in a fierce struggle for existence.

Your monuments are rusted with unfulfilled desires.
What shall we say to those
who know righteousness?

Where is the chorus of the people?
You know those who stand proudly by the flag.
You were not born for fading away.

Phoenixes!
If there is a true patriot
you are one!

Generations forget you and we are selfish.
But you are our lost conscience.
Keeper of morality until the end of time.

By the Hudson River

In the lonely autumn evening I sit by the Hudson River and watch a passing train.
After awhile a whistle sounds along the curving pathway.

In the distance the George Washington Bridge is decorated with sparkling headlights
from the vehicles that are lined up bumper to bumper on the road.

The river currents heave and set.
I see a shooting star for a fleeting moment.

How many evenings have I sat alone on this bank, watching the river's panorama!
If there were no whistles here or headlights or stars, what a desolate place before me.

But the river flows, trains run, and meteors fall.
I too drift and surge.
Sending my yearning for my home country, to and fro.

The Train Whistle

Because New Jersey's Harrington Park is awakened from its deep slumber
early mornings by the train whistle
there is no need to set an alarm for rising.

The train's shriek causes a stampede of livestock and birds
and other creatures emerge from the forest.
Then the sparrows, hares, and deer are awakened.

Though it is noisy, sometimes this distant shrill sound
creates a longing in me for my home country.

Where poor inhabitants, with no watches to guide them, welcome the useful whistle—
informing them what time to have lunch at a farm field far away,
when to dwell and leave again.

The trains pass through the forest and the villages
every day,
in all seasons.

The whistle blows:
Choo-choo, Choo-choo,
Toot-toot, Toot-toot...

Nightmare

When I sit on the bank of the Hudson River,
it blows a squall
and the river is roaring and tumultuous.

Two large dragons with long horns come out of the water,
very ugly and lean, fiercely fighting with each other,
their mouths fully open.

And as I look more closely
two small frogs, fat and sleek
are seated on the horns of each dragon.

When the monsters shrink to the size and shape of a bean
the frogs swallow them whole.
First the sleek one, then the fat one.

Now a shiny frog sits on my upper eyelids and cries all night long,
frequently crossing from my right eye to my left.
Suddenly the frog is dressed in spots of white and green.

Each time he cries, a white balloon, bigger than his entire body
inflates and deflates in his mouth.
As its red tongue repeatedly darts in and out.

Suddenly he slurps my body down inside his mouth!
I utter a full-throated shriek at the frightening sound,
as my wife wakes me with an equally shrill loudness.

A Place Where Clouds Are Flowing

On a grassy knoll by the Hudson River, I lie down with my head on my arms.
To the west many clouds are floating about
at the mercy of the wind.

An airplane is flying high through the clouds; my eyes follow it.
My yearning is wafted on the breeze
and chases the clouds.

I long to fly far off
where clouds go.

The clouds that seem to beckon with hands,
the clouds I wish to follow.

Hoping to visit a beatific place
like a childhood dream.

My imaginings take me to a land
over the continent, across the ocean.

To my beloved homeland
where I first fell in love.

So over the clouds
like a flower that blossoms
I send my love.

In a Blacksmith Shop

The dragon tattoos on the solid muscles of both forearms come alive
as the blacksmith shapes a sharp knife on the anvil.

With the might of his strong arms
he manages skillfully with one hand holding a tong,
the other a hammer, as steel yields.

At first when steel enters the blacksmith shop it is cold and stiff.
But on the anvil even stubborn and wild steel has no choice
but to succumb.

After getting red in the face,
from the heat of the flames and the thrust of the hammer,
the steel becomes a milder character.

At one time, both anvil and hammer were wild steel.
But now they are producing useful things
together with their master.

Summer High Noon

Abandoned asphalt streets in New York City—nobody walks.
I look out the window where the air shimmers with intense and stifling heat.
The pendulum of the cuckoo clock strikes two.
Everyone in the office slacks off.

A black cat awakens, pulls at his whiskers,
opens its jaws in a teeth-baring yawn,
arches its back,
then lies down with outstretched front paws.

The murderous heat comes roll by roll.
Descending like the grasshoppers that invade the streets.
Like a film of gossamer, heat winds around my arm.

Too hot, I don't know whether I breathe or not.
Vigorous heat attacks me thoroughly, through eyes, mouth, armpit and groin.
Uncountable rolls of wrapping heat seal up whole cities.

Sign Language

There are few passengers in the afternoon
on the New York City subway.

Save for three young men debating heatedly.
Hands in motion like conductors leading a symphony.

From hands and fingers their words come spewing out rapidly—
soundless into the empty space around them.

Sometimes the men seem to have passionate arguments—
wielding actions that are fast and wide.

They draw circles or straight-lines into the empty air.
Clench their fists or open them frequently.

Loosening their hands,
offering encouragement or warning—

I don't know what they are communicating.
But their soundless controversy is continuous.

Pedestrian Crosswalk at Time Square

I'm waiting for the traffic light to change to green.
People swarm around me…
clamoring to cross the busy street
within the seven seconds mandated by a machine.

They walk with hurried steps—
students with their smartphones, heads down, watch their screens;
young couples hug, slap and tickle each other;
a whistling young man pulls at his jeans.

A middle-aged woman clutches a purse in one hand and a fox terrier in another;
an elderly man, wearing large sunglasses hobbles slowly,
while a girl in a wheelchair moves determinedly.

To get to the other side they must move forward quickly—
Going with the flow…moving forward….just forward…
No option for backward motion.
Everyone moving equally.

In this short duration of time, a mass of people,
each with their own style,
moving.

The Observation Deck of the Empire State Building

The outdoor viewing area is always crowded with visitors.
Tourists gazing through the telescope to the downtown below
or scanning the distant horizon.

Couples in their wedding attire,
pose for their picture,
a bride with a bouquet by the safety fence.

Fathers carry their children on their shoulders
to show them the view
far off into the streets.

One man stands vertically on his friend's shoulder
to see the world from a more high ranking position.

An acrobatic teenager stands upright atop his friend's head.
Stretching his arms he shouts loudly:
 "I am the tallest man in the universe."

Just at that moment a nearby seagull is startled by the sound
and flying away toward the blue sky
evacuates uncontrollably on the deck floor.

Times Square

A crowded Starbucks has no seats for its customers.
Outside I drink my coffee standing—
a temporary stage in Times Square filled with all kinds of people.

I observe tourists in the busy street: a large crowd jumbled together.
Storytellers, young folks snapping pictures,
an accordion player passing his hat for money,
a bride and bridegroom at their wedding ceremony.

From where I stand it looks like they are all leading incredibly busy lives,
hurrying in step to the building's neon advertisement
that also moves ceaselessly.

Perhaps these people feel as if they are traveling together,
as if they are bewitched
by the flashing pace of billboards.

Among them only the yellow cabs move lazily
through the scurrying crowd of fast walkers.

Cigarette Butts

Scattered at random on the ground.
Each body crumpled with different forms.

Broken and cracked.
The numerous teeth marks
and lipstick stains remain

ugly on the bodies.
Marks on marks,
scars on scars.

Enduring the pain of constant biting.
Keeping all of the stories of hardship within,
their small bodies never forgetting.

Once the smokers' best friends,
They are now weltered and trampled
by pedestrians.

Cigarettes made dizzy by smoke from cherry lips,
fascinated with fragrances.
They gave fealty to their master.

Gone now.
Cast off!

They are quietly waiting
to decompose.
Perhaps strike up again.

Diving

Because it is too hot, I eat a lot of cold watermelon
adjust my easy chair all the way back
take a rest while listening to classical music.

We fling off our clothes—even our underpants—and dive into the river.
The water so soothing cool and crystal clear
we can see the bottom.

I am swimming with dear old friends
who live in the rural village
of my homeland in Korea.

We have a contest to see who will be the first to cross the river,
who can stay longest under water without breathing,
who is the fastest, strongest, the one with most endurance.

I climb a rock near the river
spread out my arms like an angel
and leap off.

I fall down
bumping my head
on the carpeted floor
of my living room.

The Rosary

In the relics' exhibition of the antiquated abbey, a rosary is displayed.
All beads threaded onto a string at regular distances;
tight knots of the cord decoupled so there is an intimacy among the bodies of the beads.

Faded beads show traces of the time and tide.
Well-thumbed wooden beads shine in dim light.
Gold beads seem to murmur something I cannot comprehend.

Alongside these compelling strands my eyes alight upon a woman's portrait.
Though she is gone, her boundless prayers seem to continue through the ages.

These beads—like a life partner—cherish many of her wishes,
remember the fervent prayers spoken during worship to her God.
Perhaps her earnest desires not only came to nothing, but were returned with despair.

If the beads spoke to me they would tell of the many tears that appeared in her eyes.
How a new crucifix attached to the rosary was bright when she first used it—
Then suddenly, beads are left alone, abandoned.

At the Margaret Mitchell House in Atlanta

Under the calm light her framed picture kindly welcomes visitors.
A typewriter holds a paper with words captured on half a page.

Cannons from the Civil War faintly thunder from the old machine.
But those sounds are drowned out for a time by a guide who recounts her life.

I meet Scarlet O'Hara in another hanging picture frame.
She welcomes me with a smile; seems to say that tomorrow is another day.

I nod gently to the portrait,
fighting the impulse to wind the spring that would awaken the old phonograph player.

The bed and sofa in the room hint of the leisure in her life.
The cooking pots, spoons, forks and knives reveal the kitchen customs of those days.

In the course of looking around at the past, I wander to the exit door,
and my mind abruptly returns to the present.

At a Shopping Mall

In New York City my wife and I go together to the shopping mall.
With all its enticements
it seems to be waiting for customers.

We are poor country people though.
Not familiar with malls.
So we step slowly through the stores.

We push our large cart and look
with our eyes opened wide…
hunting for a discount corner
to purchase goods with a big sale price.

My wife shows an interest in buying kitchen appliances—
white porcelain tea pots, pottery jars and stainless steel pans.
Items she always longed to have
in our kitchen at home in Korea.

But on this occasion I try to calm her earnest desires.
Telling her that we could buy
the more expensive items
next time.

Then my wife scolds me vehemently
about a next time that is coming continually
again and again
and never arrives.

Aged Dartboard at the Flea Market

Every Saturday I visit the flea market.
Even when snow flurries slide in through the open showcase.
Every gust of wind shaking the portable tent, the old Lespedeza door.

Today I find an aged dartboard hung on a makeshift wall.
Its surface color faded and partially flaked off.
Most of the numbers only dimly visible.

There are places that illustrate the history
where passionate players once competed.
Aiming the dart at the marked lucky numbers to win the game.

But the board holds both lucky and unlucky numbers
and though everyone sets sights on the inner bull's-eye
it is difficult to hit the mark.

Now remember the players of long ago,
their jubilant and wistful smiles, win or lose.
Now the old salesman's wrinkled face

feels the cold winds passing through
the lonely ether.

Journey With No Definite Objective

In a rural park I sit on a sloped wooden bench,
make a pillow of my arm for my head,
gaze up at the distant sky, lost in thought.

There are nine hundred lambs and one thousand swans
walking at a leisurely pace in line across the sky.
A faint crescent moon hangs between them.

A shepherd in white clothes with a staff in his hand follows slowly.
Sometimes the staff pokes its head into the crescent
pulling it up toward the herd of lambs.

There is no traffic cop or expert to expedite these movements,
to make sure that everything flows harmoniously.

Two groups of white birds high in the sky turn round and round,
their feathers floating on wind that seems lighter than air.

All of them drift toward me—lambs, swans and birds.
Balanced buoyantly on a journey
with no definite objective.

Panorama of the Streets

Autumn breezes
blow the yellow leaves
off the roadside trees.
They scatter on the asphalt pavement.

A surging crowd of leaves are rambling through the streets
according to the winds.
They all fade to a similar color,
trampled down by shoes and tires recklessly.
My trousers brush past some of these lean leaves.

No one shows an interest in them.
Except an old woman at the bus stop
examining them carefully.
She seems to long for the vibrant colors and glorious times
of the past.

In the street so many people gather.
The surging crowds are moved around
here and there, according to the traffic lights.

Where do they come from? When?
How long will they be wandering from place to place?
Did the leaves, like them, have days of youth?

The buses come and go.
The old woman departs and others appear.
Afterward autumn leaves disappear from here.
The roadside trees will come into bud next spring.

In the night the crowds will be buried in darkness.
What is seen today is gone with the night.
Yet the panorama of the streets of New York
will remain with me for a long time to come.

On Breezy Waikiki Beach

The rainbows sing.
Sky is high through a rift in the clouds.
Too many waves to count.
Too much sand to count.
Too many days to count.

White birds skim over the sea.
Sailboards skim the calm sea.
So many colorful parasols!
Young people surfing.
Bikini-clad sunbathers.

While waves talk with sand,
rainbows, clouds, and wind,
Hawaiians drum and dance.
Like sighing for the good old days
the stories are continued with murmuring waves.

If I were wind I could hear you.

If I should meet you again after a long time, Waikiki,
how should I greet you?

Dream of a Marathon Runner

Marathon athletes at the starting line
in the bright sunshine
of the London 2012 Olympics.
Ready to run the course:
past Buckingham Palace, St. Paul's Cathedral, the Tower of London.

Tagged on their front and rear with a name and an ID number.
After long hard years of training
they stand
as representatives
of their country.

As soon as the signal is sounded
their journey begins.
Sturdy legs propel them
toward the finish line.
They compete.
Hoping to accomplish a dream.

At the signal
some runners rush forward
to the head of the pack.
But their lead begins to shrink
after half the course is run.

The day grows hotter.

Some runners drink too much water
from the bottles offered along the way.

Some runners look often at their watches.
Only at last to give up on their journey.

Although racing brings their bodies together,
the struggle for survival is a solitary pursuit.

One runner controls his pace with precision—
suddenly surges ahead in the final stages of the race.
Leaping like a stag from inside the pack
to the front position.

Winning the race.
He becomes the gold medalist.
Draped in his country's flag.

At the finish line
the last runner to cross
tells the press,
"The journey is more important
than the medals.
Never giving up along the way,
is the final achievement."

Dreaming Each Day

What did you do today? If you ask me this, I did nothing.
What did you do today? If you ask again, I did too much.
I do something every day, but don't know exactly what it is.
I do nothing every day, but too busy always.

What do I gain day-to-day? I don't know.
The sun rises and the sun sets, but I don't perceive it.
There are so many stars in the sky, but I cannot count them,
unless I let myself fall into evening.

Waves in the ocean, sands on the beach, leaves in the forest,
days of our life,
How many numbers are they?
Is it utterly meaningless to talk about?

In order to know them, I'm living.

I get up every morning,
work for my livelihood, and
I cultivate myself each day.

Descartes said, *I think, therefore I am*, and they are.
From nine to five, morning to evening,
I am wasting away outwardly, but
I am renewed inwardly day by day.

Even though I am a mist that appears
for a little while and vanishes,
I don't lose heart.

For my light and momentary troubles
are ripening
a beautiful dream.

I cultivate myself each day.
I dream the dream each day.

Refugees

Like fallen leaves that sway in the wind
shadowed by scattered clouds
we wander from place to place
taking steps wherever our legs might carry us.

Not staying regularly in any one place
we never know where we should stop for sleep.
We are afraid of darkness.

We never knew that people could be so callous
the morning dew so cold
and early frost is hard as stone.

In the old days we didn't recognize
that worthless fog was important—
wrapping us out of sight
creating a kindly feeling
even though we shivered with cold.

We are fallen leaves
discarded by trees
in front of our own houses—

Houses that are run down and abandoned.
Leaves that are strewn about by the winds.

Last Hope for Dream

What force causes a young boy to be drowned at sea?
The image on my T.V. captures him face down in the sand,
broken waves sweeping over him continuously.

Refugees in mass migrations—
like butterflies or birds, tenuous, fragile,
resting in the streets, frantic facing starvation
or arrest by militia.

A young child walks barefoot over cold stone slabs.
A mother with belongings bundled on her head
holds a child in each hand.
These Internet images I see…

Desperate to cross a border of mesh wire fence
into neighboring country or further
guarded by frontier garrison
pushed back, brutally beaten.

Even though they are hard-pressed on every side
they fix their dream not on what is seen
but on what is unseen.

An Empty Space

When a woman volunteer approaches an orphan at the refugee village
a boy opens his arms and tightly hugs her.

Like a magnet the boy clings to her and won't let go.
Other orphans clamber to her, but there is no room for them.

Watching this on my television screen
I see a huge unfilled place between them.

And the empty spaces in the eyes of each orphan
like an abyss of sorrow and despair.

Who can make smaller
these barren spaces between them?

III.

The Seasons Have Gone But....

The seasons revolve,
and the years change unconsciously
without asking or notice.

The light green grass in the fields that comes up through the ground decorates the
wildflowers. The shimmering spring heat waving in the air
helps bloom the flowers of the peach and azalea.
Will my hometown also bloom by now?

The town I lived in was the flowering mountain in the spring.
Even though I now live in distant lands far away,
the flowers that bloom in my heart are aflutter with the idea of returning there.

You were only laughing silently about that time;
the petals of those days were tinted with shyness.
Though far away, it continues to haunt me.

The seasons, without taking thought,
revolve in cycles—spring, summer, autumn, and winter.
The seasons that have been forgotten
have come back with nostalgia,
and you are full in my heart of vast vacancy.

The turning seasons each time put fire on the wick of a forgotten longing.
Past seasons have gone,
but those days remain in my heart.

My heart set on what I have been longing for,
while the moon moves in its cycle—crescent, half moon, full.
The flower petals too have bloomed and fallen
but your shy smile is unchanged.

Opening Night, Predawn Morning

In the new opera house, so elegant and clean,
my wife and I sit together.
My heart flutters in anticipation.

We are so poor we can only afford seats under the balcony.
Our view is obscured, but it is enough that we can still fly away to curious countries
through the stories conjured during the performance.

The orchestra's overture blares out
toward both sides of the curtain moving slowly.
And the brilliant stars on stage lead us to a new world.

Before daylight on the mountain in the foreground of my village
the merry chatter of the sparrows
wake the livestock and the reed forest from a sound sleep.

With each new day I always expect a new possibility.
The curtain of night pulling back, a radiant sun dawning over the mountain ridge
inch by inch, opening up a new world brightly.

A world that I sincerely welcome
each new day
with my arms open wide
taking a bow, receiving applause.

Arirang

With much mirth at the party we are singing Arirang.
"Why are you always singing Arirang?" our children ask.
"Because it heals our nostalgia for our homeland."

"Arirang arirang arariyo,
my love heartlessly goes over the Arirang hill
in spite of my earnest request for her to stay,

but my love might not make it even one mile,
because of getting ill, getting ill
before my love reaches there, reaches there"

The Arirang song; our unofficial national anthem,
our favorite chorus, our best friend and coordinator
in the people's party of the homeland.

"Arirang arirang arariyo...,
you go over, you go over
Arirang hill

My love, you leave me, you leave me,
your feet will be sore, your feet will be sore
before you go one mile..."

We begin to dance a Korean folk dance
to the melody of the Arirang...
We dance with both hands,

sometimes holding a handkerchief in one hand,
the other hand resting on the waist,
dancing forward and backward repeatedly.

We toast to our success and health.
We form a ring and dance, again and again and again...
we spin right to left, then the opposite way, singing the chorus merrily.

"Arirang arirang arariyo, Arirang arirang arariyo,
you should not leave me, not leave me
you should not leave me, not leave me"

* **"Arirang"** is a Korean folk song, often considered the unofficial national anthem of Korea. There are about 3,600 variations of 60 different versions of the song, all of which include a refrain similar to, *Arirang, arirang, arariyo.* It is estimated the song is more than 600 years old.

Flower Watch

I return to my home country of Korea—
Walk along the riverside where clovers grow
where Seunee and I played together as children.
We were poor, but happy.

Sometimes we squatted in the clover fields
searching for four-leaf clovers all day long
—believing it might bring us luck.
But it was not easy to find this treasure.

Sometimes we bet on who would discover a four-leaf clover first;
but Seunee always won.
Sometimes she asked me to sing to her or kiss her cheek.
Or make a watch from the clover flowers to adorn her wrist.

At first I didn't know how to create this thing.
But I soon realized that to make one watch
two flowers must be equally joined together.

Now I stand alone in the vast clover plains
in the dusk where flowers are in full bloom.
I call for Seunee loudly, but there is no answer.
Only a lonely echo.

At the Gate

I stop by chance at the gate of my childhood home.
It is dusk. More than fifty years have passed away.

I can only see the roof of the house that is surrounded by a high wall,
and I don't know who is living there.

Now I imagine that someone is about to come running to me.
Shouting my name for joy.

The thatched roof has been tiled
and the wooden fence—overgrown with clover—
has become a blunt concrete wall.

Inside the courtyard, the Evergreens have disappeared
and the cold wind sweeps through its empty space.

I hesitate a moment, deliberate, whether to push the gate's bell.
Then I give up and close my eyes. Sit with my back against the wall.

Now childhood friends are singing the folk ballads of long ago.
The songs echo through the icicles hanging from the eaves of the straw roof.

One by one the faces of loved ones flash through my mind.
Those good old days have ascended high up into the sky
and dispersed like meteors.

Come Back Soon

Wed during the Korean War,
a marriage night of ecstasy, the nuptial bed, a bliss…
and at that very moment an explosion.

Startled, the bridegroom cries out!
Sweeps aside his bride, leaving her behind in the room.
Saying, "I'll come back soon."

She firmly believes that he will be back at once.
Remains awake all night waiting.
Although no information ever comes,
the bride waits for him, faithfully.

She remains in their old house,
not moving to another place, or city.
Not wanting to repair anything broken,
even to exchange the gate for a new one.

She fears that her husband might not recognize the house
with its thatched straw roof
that they had entered
the first night of matrimony.

Almost sixty years later,
the old bridegroom visits his hometown on business
after getting government approval.

By now he has forgotten his first wife
but still curious about the old house
he stops there spontaneously.

When she opens the door, the old bride recognizes her husband.
Her heart flutters greatly.
She becomes a white balloon.

And when the old bridegroom touches her
her heart fills with so much compassion
she floats up into the sky.

While a man,
a perfect image of a bridegroom
stands at the doorstep.

Chuseok

When I leave my homeland, it is late summer; during the days of Chuseok,
a national holiday, the Korean Thanksgiving.

When I am reminded of the old days,
I think of the full moon rising above the hills of my hometown.

Smiling alone while in a small park I fall into memories of Chuseok Eve;
in the cobalt sky the full moon is always smiling for us.

My friends and I make a campfire, sing a folk song together;
We form a ring and the girls dance Ganggangsulae.

Hand in hand, spinning right to left, or opposite,
singing the chorus merrily.

At midnight we eat Songpyeon,
rice cakes stuffed with chestnuts and sesame, and topped with honey.

I open my eyes and walk across the village square.
A pedestrian holding a bouquet of pale violet lilacs,
and I think of the coming full moon days.

Hometowns Are Passing

Through the windows of the airplane our hometowns are passing away:
The school buildings with their wide grounds,
and the high belfry of the church,
the spacious golden autumn field,
the mounds and hills and even mountain ranges,
together with a river, are moving farther away.

Suddenly memories of my childhood appear out of the passing.
Like watching a movie backward I see:
a one-room house with a thatched roof in the country,
six children sleeping in one-room that has no bed,
father on the right side and mother on the left,
only one blanket between us.

In that small and narrow space I dreamt I was a bird flying free.
Now, on a plane leaving my hometown,
even if the panorama on the ground below disappears
these childhood memories do not leave me.

Kimchi

Although memories of my hometown are increasingly forgotten,
my favorite Korean food is still in my heart.
How I crave Kimchi!

I cannot forget its characteristic smell—its scallions, ginger and garlic.

The old days are dim, but the longing for this taste continues;
fresh Kimchi on a picnic, fermented Kimchi after a long journey,
mellow-radish Kimchi late at night when the snow is blowing.

In pouring rain or heavy snow I used to drive long distances for Kimchi.

Now I sit under the lamplight with a grey-haired childhood chum.
In the dusk of early evening we watch the full moon rise over the mountain.
Old days have gone by, but my taste for Kimchi is with me, like an old friend.

Hammer and Sickle

The scars on my left fingers remind me of my childhood.
During the Korean War we were poor and miserable.
Hungry, I wandered the streets to find food.

Sometimes, even though I was a very young boy, I worked at construction sites,
using a hammer to break stones into small pieces for the concrete bridges.

Sometimes I was careless and the hammer hit my finger.
Each time the wounds took longer to heal.

In summer I went out to the fields to cut fodder for compost,
mowing grass with a sickle and repeatedly injuring my fingers.

The hammer and sickle were my familiar childhood friends,
teaching me the sanctity of bread, rest and freedom.

Too Late

In late spring she called, asking me softly, with kindness in her voice,
"Come to my home to play before the cherry blossoms fall."
"I'll try my best," I said, but never went after all.

Even forgetting her name for a long time after.

One dark winter night I visit with a white chrysanthemum.
While driving to her, Beethoven's Symphony No.5 flows from the car radio,
petals from the chrysanthemum and seeds of balsam flowers pour out onto the seat.

The seeds seem to breathe, the buds rise, and soon the red-colored flowers bloom clearly;
I dye her fingernails with the petals of garden balsams,
then her face is wreathed in smile.

In spite of myself, days come and go quickly.

Many friends and acquaintances attend the send-off ceremony of her spirit.
In front of her portrait there is a black rosary and many flowers.
I place a white chrysanthemum before her.

The Sorrow

I'm at the window with the green tea she sent me.
I'm drinking the leisure hour of the afternoon
contained wholly in the tea
that has brewed little by little.

The sorrow spreads silently like a shadow
and drifts like a wind.
Appearing unexpectedly from time to time
though it never seems to stand in the way of the wide steps of life.

Now it comes together
with the fragrance of the tea.
Then ebbs from me.

Like a mass of dough in the hands of a baker.
Could I knead this sorrow till it is pliable?
Or like soft down on a thistle
it possible for it to blow away completely?

While I drink slowly
she is with me silently.
Spreads over the quiet surface of the cup with fragrance
and slips into my heart.

Storyline

In the picture his eyes are smiling as before.
But she still has a heart fraught with sorrow.
It might take more time to leave this love.

First thing in the morning she greets him.
And each day when she leaves for the office
he see her off from his place in the family room.

When she comes back home she tries not to spend so much time there,
decreasing the length of her conversations with him.
She waits for the day she will forget what might have been fruitful; but it is not easy.

The smile in the gilt-framed picture contains all of the stories:
that discourse about the operas
that she used to watch with him.

But there is no sound from the photo.
Now he seems to be
keeping silence.

Yet he is still smiling
and her fruit is yet ripe.
Although the framed picture
is covered with dust.

Seollal

The Lunar New Year's Day, Seollal, always brings nostalgia;
sometimes I return to my hometown in Korea.
We were poor, but happy together
and always had a good time during Seollal.

Sometimes we eat *Tteokuk*, Korea's traditional Sliced Rice Cake Soup,
or wear *Hanbok*, Korea's traditional dress, and visit friends and relatives.
The children bow to the adults and receive their cash gifts,
and play *Yutnori*, a customary board game;
usually I am disqualified but not displeased.

Sometimes I visit our ancestors' graves to pay my respects to them,
and to the old places with the children to learn our history.
Sometimes, in the winter season I play ski
while coming down along the ridge of the mountain
or sleigh ride along the freezing river.
Some winter seasons great flakes of snow continue falling day and night for several days,
and then the whole town is buried.

Now, in San Francisco, I get out of my car for a walk alone on Seollal
and I stand on a trail in the hills at dusk.
A boy is flying a colorful kite
and the western skies are lit up with the glow of the setting sun.

The red tail of the kite flickers in the soft breeze
It seems to beckon me to follow.
Suddenly memories of childhood come back in rapid succession,
like the rising tide.

I send greetings to my homeland
through the kite's string that might be extended to there.

Under the Old Pine

I read my friend's letter under the old pine tree—it's similar to the pine at hometown
that looks like a big mushroom or huge umbrella to shelter me.
The trunk of the tree shows the motion of time, but its needles remain green.

The pine tree standing regally in the back woods of my hometown
was the guardian of our neighborhood. As a young boy, I played hide and seek
with my childhood friends around the pine tree and dreamed my dreams.

Now I stand, leaning back on the trunk of the old pine tree in New York's Central Park.
Homesick for those days, I play the harmonica to relieve nostalgia, sing a folk song
continuously, and call my childhood friend's name repeatedly.

Under the old pine tree
I write a letter to my dear friend.
And a pleasant childhood day comes back to me.

Now what do I gain from my labor at which I toil here?
While I didn't notice that the sun rose and set, then hurried back to where it rose again,
my hair has been turning grey.

All things are like the clouds in the sky that appear for awhile and vanish.
Like chasing after wind,
nothing is gained here.

This winter may also pass soon
and the spring disappear;
the summer too will vanish and then this year.

I'd like to gather up my things and
head back to my hometown.
What do I gain from my labor at which I toil here?
While writing my letter

the full moon rises far away above the horizon.
The same moon my friend may also see under the old tree there.

Light and Shadow

Her brown hair flutters in the gentle breeze.
Shining in the sunlight—dancing a dance of the zephyr.

She sleeps on her fiancé's shoulder.
Her mouth open
as if she is singing a solo.

Tangled hair, no make-up, no lipstick
her breasts exposed.

In this manner, ugliness is exchanged for beauty—
the intelligence of her fiancé for her own shortcomings.
Her dreams are hers but outside of her.

Light pours in through the crevices of the clouds,
scurries across her.
Then the shadow of a cloud.

But it doesn't concern her
that the light and shadow come and go
while she sleeps.

Or that the weather will cycle clear and cloudy
at irregular intervals.
Or that their abiding hour is fleeting.

Faded Letter

While putting my desk in order
I stumbled across a faded letter.

It seemed I wrote it a long time ago,
But now I no longer understand the words.

Vestiges of adolescence hang in the sky;
as a young yellow-colored butterfly.

I had painted a rainbow-colored dream on paper
and was delighted with you.

But even now you are bringing me flowers.
A floral perfume
that emanates from the drawings.

Like a hieroglyphic letter from ancient people
this becomes a legendary story.

At the moment I put the letter into the drawer
I see a butterfly float aimlessly away
outside my window.

White Porcelain Vase

On a small table in the corner of a Buddhist altar
sits a white porcelain vase.
How long has it been there I wonder?

The moonlight flows together with a stream
in the black and white painting.
Two carps meet where the gentle waves
approach the side of the frame.

The warm sunshine enters the room
through the windows covered with Oriental paper.
The sunshine brightens the room and the full moon in the painting.
From another room, a wooden gong sounded by a priest is heard faintly.

The bell permeates the empty void
softly filling the room fully.
Pushes me to renounce my mundane agonies
and flow along with the stream in the painting
of the antique white porcelain vase.

After awhile the windows are opened slightly.
Outside the dried leaves are scattered on the ground
by the brisk wind.

Bronze Image of Buddha

On an open corner
at the Asian Art Museum in San Francisco,
a bronze Buddha is attentively listening, despite a crowd of visitors.

He doesn't care about me. Yet I approach him.
Up close I see that his ears are open to the outside:
the clamor made by men and women, the earth, sky, clouds, and wind…
all things in nature.

Finally, after a long time
these reverberations mingle together
and are heard simply as one sound.

The Buddha's dark-gray complexion shows me an eternity.
He seems to laugh at me,
enduring this waiting, endeavoring to be humble.

With eyes slightly open and grasping another's hand in front,
He is endlessly and eagerly listening,
seeking the noise from outside.

I close my eyes and calmly review days past.

For the Chrysanthemum

When other flowers fall in autumn
she blooms alone.

Despite frosty mornings,
her work is to become glorious petals.
And the air is laden with the scent of chrysanthemums.

In order to come into bloom
the chrysanthemum endures
scorching heat that confines her for days in summer.

She hears rolls of thunder in the distance
and feels heavy showers falling whole days.

She sees flocks of swans fly away through dark clouds before sunset.
She is cultivated from gentle breezes in the mountains.

In her short life, the chrysanthemum has experienced prosperity and adversity.
Once the chrysanthemums are fallen, no other flowers remain.

I pray to God, I wish not to follow her too soon
into the dark and cold winter night.

Unknown Flowers in the Valley

The flowers bloom.
The flowers bloom.
The unknown flowers bloom
in the valleys of the mountain
from spring to summer.

Because of loving the silence,
the flowers bloom alone.
The flowers bloom lonely
among the weeds
in the secluded valleys.

Because of loving the sun,
the flowers bloom from day to day.
The unknown flowers bloom
from day to day continually.

Because of not wanting
to show their shabby leaves,
the flowers fade away in the evening.
The flowers fade away together with the wind.
The unknown flowers vanish away silently.

While Sweeping the Leaves in My Back Yard

In autumn I sweep the leaves every day.
There are many kinds of deciduous trees
older than neighboring evergreens.

In spring, these trees come into leaf at different times,
but descend in autumn simultaneously
after the color has faded.

In summer, the leaves grow luxuriantly
taking various shapes that cast shadows
that block the glaring sunlight at noon
and call up mysterious forest spirits and creatures
on a windy evening.

In frosty autumn, once upright and prosperous leaves
hang their browning heads down.
The fallen leaves lie down together in the recesses, living together peacefully.

I sweep the leaves together.
Assembling them into piles outside my yard.
To be taken away by the garbage truck in the morning.

Growth Ring

In the front yard of my house
stand several large maples.
Taller than all the others
in the neighborhood.

As soon as they appear ready to bud in spring
I take notice.
Watch intently each day as the leaves grow luxuriantly.
Finally forming a dense, gloomy thicket in summer.

My windows look out into the garden, and
even though I take tea every day
seeing the same trees outside
I do not anticipate them turning with autumn's color.

Many squirrels live in these trees.
Spending their time scurrying up and down.
Once one, while going down, suddenly stopped
to look at me, his eyes meeting mine.

After a meal in the dining room
I climb the stairs to my second floor study,
and a squirrel also goes up to the top,
by way of the trunk of the tree.

The maple leaves, now brown, have fallen.
In such a short time the trees have become scrawny.

When evening falls all things
are covered with darkness.
Another morning is preparing to be opened.
Each day is just like every other day.

The squirrels and I travel up and down
and the tree's growth ring increases annually.

The Last Leaf of Autumn

All, all are left but one;
the last lonely leaf swaying in cold winds.

Showing her silvery underside;
destined to come down soon.

All her lovely companions
have faded away.

The branches of the trees are thin—
their leaves all vanished.

Hour by hour it grows colder.
Just before sunset the clouds drop down.

Like the leaf,
I almost fall fluttering in the wind.

Like the leaf, I nearly fall fluttering
from the branches of myself.

In days past I missed out on something spiritual.
And I wasted time and effort.

If I were a balmy breeze I'd talk with her.
If I were a swift cloud I'd fly to former days.

I will not leave her to waste on the branch.
All will join me in singing her praises.

Ripened Pumpkin

Loose and abundant woman.
Woman of lenient mind
lying on the sofa.

She offers comfort
and humor
I rest in her sunny smile.

Innocent, round, nude.
Fattened from soil
and earth.

The Heavy Snow, The Chaos

I

All day, every day, the snow is falling ceaselessly;
Until all things on the earth are covered with snow.
And due to severe
descending
snow
visibility is nearly zero.
It seems that a piece of the heavens has quietly opened,
failing to control the quantities of snow falling to earth.
Or perhaps after being scolded by the heavens
the clouds work off their vexations with heavy snowfall…
Like a master kicking a dog who has disobeyed.

II

At the first snow day, the yards and roads were slightly covered
with light and soft snowflakes.
Everything was rounded off, smoothed over, magnificently.
However, the next day, the true character of the snowflakes was revealed.
Then they submerged the alleys and cars nearly to their windows,
broke the trees and roofs of barns.
Piled up snow closed the doors of houses and stores.
Now confines all citizens to their homes.
The city was put out of commission by the snow.

III

The snow, although trampled and humbled,
still behaves perversely.

One Freezing Day

Minus twenty-one degrees Celsius this morning—
The mountains, rivers, lakes, trees, and even myself, are frozen over.

In freezing days such as these
I imagine
descending
into the earth
and living there
together
with roots.

And even though the earth is frozen with ice
and all the grasses are withered,
I will hear the murmuring
of the brooks that flow
through the numerous roots in the ground.
Underground tubers and bulbs preparing
for new life
with the coming spring.

And in the ground beneath
I may be invited by the moles to a New Year's Eve party.
Where warm in their burrow perhaps I will see their folk dances
that I never experienced above ground …
What genial places there are underground!

I imagine
after the winter season passes
I will return home,
together with the frogs.

The Day Is Snowing, I'm Comfortably Warm

All morning
slow clouds smoothly flying
over the front
and back yard.

For the last several days
low clouds hanging
in the foreground of the mountains.
Covered with a veil of clouds.

Day and night whole clouds
assemble in the Heavens.
Preparing great snowflakes.
Now falling softly and silently through the bare branches of trees.

It's as if someone operates a magnificent factory in the sky.
Where all kinds of clouds, long shreds and tatters of fog,
the cries of birds, and even the sound of words,
are mixed.

And stripped of color, become
these snowflakes descending to the fields.
Like green sugar cane changed
to white refined sugar in the factories.

The day is snowing, I'm comfortably warm.
Even though the weather is below freezing.
I walk up and down through the hamlet park
humming "White Christmas."

Great snowflakes are falling in the pines.
Making big snowy tassels in the boughs.

From above, the clouds are gazing on the astonishing panorama of our hamlet.
From the clouds, the snowflakes are descending continuously.

And my buoyant mind is ascending to the sky
like a balloon.

A Snowman Smiled

In the calm and emptiness of the hamlet park
a sturdy lad stands alone in front of a tall pine.
He is a horrid and ridiculous figure.

His left arm is broken.
One large eye made with charcoal and deep-black eyebrows almost gone.
A mustache made with pine needles is cut in half.
Only traces of a nose and mouth remain.

In his right hand he tightly holds an American flag,
like a soldier wounded in many battles.

I feel pity for him.

I restore his arm, eyes, eyebrows, mustache, nose and mouth.
Then after reinforcing the face and body with snowflakes,
I cover his neck with a red muffler.

I think he will be happy and smile at last.
But still he looks wooden, expressionless, lonely.
So I make another snowman exactly the same beside him.

And as I turn to head toward home
I hear a deep laughing voice at my back.

Into The Snowy Field

When he entered the university from Korea
he had no spare clothes.
Wearing dark blue jeans the first day,
and every day, until he graduated.

His classmates thought he had an obsession for jeans.
But he confided in me
that once in a while he would have liked to have worn leather pants,
a jacket with a fur lining.

After we spoke
he walked across the campus
into the field
toward the horizon
with big flakes of snow falling
as they had for several days.

After graduation we scattered.
Each to survive on our own,
out in the vast field of the world.

I saw his portrait in the paper,
set out with a border of white chrysanthemums.
I read about the car accident on the highway during a snowy winter day.

In the photo, he was wearing blue jeans.
Who else but I knew?
How he wished to wear the warmth of leather in cold weather.

Fish Sleep

The fish in the Chinese supermarket stare up at the customers.
While the salesman touts their stellar attributes, fish eyes glare.

The fish on the grill stare up at the cook.
Out of the burning fire their eyes glower.

Like singers their mouths are fully opened,
but without the blinking eyes of chorus members.

When they were caught by the fisherman's casting net
they strongly refused; opening their mouth to feed one last time.
As the air tightened around the fish gills…as death approached finally.

The fire burns the fish, eyes still wide open.
Eyes that have no eyelids.
Eyes that neither sleep nor death can close.

When fish sleep the wide Pacific lays a blanket over them.
The sea sings a lullaby to sleep.

While the fish burn on the grill, no one listens.
But the fish mouths are still wide open.

As if they had all joined in singing
the blue waves of the sea.

Ice Trout Fishing

There is a tense moment
felt between what's above the ice and what's below.
Only the fishing line serves as an intermediary.

Dim and far from man's reach,
in the deep part of the lake where trout live.
Where hunger stares him in the face.

While keeping quiet beneath thick ice;
always anxious about news on the surface.
What goes on there?

In a slight tent the fisherman spends three days.
Bores a small hole through the ice.
Drops the fishing line with night crawlers on an angler's hook.
Still no biting signal.

Below,
the trout keep their full attention on the delicious smelling bait.
Ecstasy and uncertainty—their appetite, leading them into temptation.

Above,
strong cold ennui for the fisherman.
A parallel tension between trout and man.

View of the Thawing

Thawing snow runny like rice gruel.
As the poor city streets
regain their original appearance.

Boarded up houses, decrepit from lack of care, show their fatigue.
The leaking roofs repaired with plastic sheets
to protect them from relentless rain.

Sidewalks, forcibly awakened from slumber,
now exposed to a medley of noises from cars, children, loudspeakers.
Sidewalks, previously embedded in snow, revealed.
Heaped with trash and dogs' dung, miscellaneous fluids…

The face of the city, fair-skinned, like an imperial princess.
Thawing, slushy, soppy.
Her snowy makeup rapidly effaced by a spring breeze.

Glasses In Winter

It is minus degrees and cloudy.
It feels like it could snow.

The bus stop at the early commuter hour is teeming
with the salaried workers standing in line.
Waiting—I am one of them.

I get on the Number 7 bus, as I do every morning.
But suddenly my view is blocked entirely.

I flounder at the threshold.
Then, like a blind man
stumble to find a seat.

But there is no way to see.
Until the vapor curtain from the outside is drawn back.

I never expected this invisible enemy.
Hiding in the air, attacking my glasses.
Over the wide differences of temperature and humidity.

Abundant Dreaming Palace

The tinged autumnal leaves build a palace in paradise.
A palace that is full of laughter and music for all eternity.
A place where there is no sickness or death.
These autumnal leaves warm my heart and comfort me.

The hills are ablaze with striking color for one week only.
The palace in paradise is hung in the sky.
There is no admission fee to enter
and everyone is welcome to live here.

In the middle of the autumn season
with its ripening fruits and grains
I would like to live in this dreaming palace
for the duration of the season.

IV.

Sunset

A man whose face blushes up to the roots of his hair
is passing beyond the western hill.
Empty handed, not carry anything.
He is always alone.

Hurrying to pass
as if late for an engagement,
he is counseled by the sparrows and the fawns
to go home early, before darkness.

Often he looks happy
with a broad smile on his face.
On these pleasant days he dyes the whole sky—even the clouds—aglow
while passing over the hill.

But when he is in poor spirits
because of his loneliness
he is not seen
for many days.

Sometimes he puts a lamp on the eastern hill
while passing beyond
and vanishes away to the western side.

While A Paper Boat Sails

I launch a folded paper boat on the stream
where a brook is murmuring down through waterweeds.

A boat I made simply, with a red mast
and the outer bottom colored sky blue.

I launch the boat into gentle waves,
but after awhile it is shaken by a breeze
and shaded by a drift of clouds.

Sometimes small fish tease the boat dangerously,
and once a ruby dragonfly landed on the top of the mast
its wings spread out, humming a barely audible song.

So the lonely night comes on.
A myriad of stars rise in the sky
and the waves lull the makeshift boat to safety.

Chopsticks

My wife and I sit together in a booth
at the bright and clean Chinese restaurant.
It is the slow hour now.

Several pairs of chopsticks are waiting
for the customers at the table.
Like troops of soldiers lined up to be inspected
they are set out in an orderly way.

A well-educated dieter, I've never hailed them.
Yet they seem to call to me...
"Hey Fatty," I hear them say.
I am anxious to be given a good name as a faithful servant.

Even though these chopsticks have much work to do
they have no grievance against the owner.
They always act in unison.
Not separately.

They do not discriminate by sex or race.
They form a perfectly equitable society of companions.

It is natural that there are keen competitions among men.
But imagine the gains made while cooperating with each other.

Prior to their work,
the chopsticks are resting for awhile together.

Painting

Sometimes the carelessly lined circle becomes a flower.
And a casually drawn horizontal line becomes the place
where Earth meets up with Heaven.

I glimpse the bony branches while I sketch…
The lines on the paper become the morning sunlight.
Or the thorns of rose bushes.

Bright flowers bloom.

The rose thorns turn into pins which pierce the fin
of the fishes like memories
that are sleeping in the deep lake.

The lilies are shy and smiling,
hiding in the woods.

I'm listening to Vivaldi's "Four Seasons."

Outside, it is raining; gusty winds whip around me.
And lightning strikes with a loud voice.

Just at that moment the electric lights go out.
Everything vanishes into the darkness.
I light a candle and start again—

Put my pencil to the blank page.

Mummy Entreats

In a showcase of dim light
her gloomy smile captivates me.
A pale ashen-brown prehistoric mummy
lies face up on a table.
Her long black hair winds around her neck
covered in a dark green linen muffler.
Discolored teeth distorted in her open mouth.
But her face has not lost its contours, its beauty once perceived.

Beside her body lies a gold chain, jade earrings and green precious stones—
objects that indicate she was a high-ranking imperial princess.
Still, from the blood stains on her ragged jacket,
I suspect her last moments were tragic
and her final cries reach out to me in the silence.

When my eyes meet her eyes she pathetically vindicates herself.
She who was falsely accused of rebellion and then died.
Regardless of the explanation I read on the display case label
she might have been wrongly accused by rogues or schemers.

In the futilities of her life sometimes there were good seasons:
When maidservants ornamented her face and body
with jewels and perfumes…
But all vanished in a moment.
Only these articles remain as eyewitness.

Imagining the last day of the princess
I am pushed from the showcase by a crowd of visitors.
Though I leave the museum, her piercing cries follow me.

Ruby

I'm reading a book on American history.
My wife's asleep
under the lamp's red-shaded glow.

On Hollywood's red carpet
Marilyn Monroe's scarlet lipstick
outlines her sunny smile. Her cheeks are rouged too.

She arranges a red ribbon in the lapel of her jacket;
wears high-heeled shoes, the color of fire.
A crimson-capped young girl presents a bouquet of burgundy roses.

Outside the Stars and Stripes wave in the wind.

Suddenly a shot is heard from a car in Dallas.
Blood, ruby-red, pours from President John F. Kennedy.

His wife, Jacqueline, cries out loudly.
Later, a single red rose is placed on the grave.

The Border

Monterey weather is calm and free.
Seaside aquarium crowded with visitors.
Schools of fish are swimming
inside the border.

A crowd of anchovy are dancing quickly like one
according to the fish trainer's intention.
No one is falling into disorder.

A sea otter's infant is playing ball,
sucking milk from his mother's breast.
The infant doesn't even know the visitors,
is not interested.

But mother sea otter looks anxious,
keeps a sharp lookout.
Her heart is outside in the immense blue ocean.

Inside, a lonely island!
Sealed despair.
Nostalgia's flag!

Tender affections keep hearts beating.
She misses her childhood in the vast ocean, her birthplace.
Never thinks of that windstorm night
when she was caught by fishermen.

In the outside border
children are chattering continually.
The youngest and the oldest are observing
inside the aquarium closely.
Infants are playing with rattles,
sucking milk from their mothers' breasts.

Everybody takes great pleasure
from the inside border.
By the fish and the sea otters' sacrifice
they are enjoying.
By another's sacrifice we are taking happiness.

Inside and outside.
Ourselves and others.
The border,
Who made it?

I Didn't Know That Before

I didn't know that before.
I never expected it before.
I didn't realize that you were going to leave
without saying a word.

So vain, how did you heartlessly leave without a sound?
Was there anything so urgent
that you could not say goodbye?

My beloved gone.

I call your name
to an empty field.
I loudly call your name out into the air.

Our firmly sworn promise
like a handful of dust
floats away in the breeze.

You appeared for a little while.
Now faded away like mist.

You'll never know I've loved you endlessly.

As you go through the years
you may repent.
Call me anytime.

Though you may look shabby,
I'll be there to wrap your broken heart.

You left, but cross-way whispers of love between us
come back
like an echo that fills a void.

Though She Left Me

Once I tried hard to escape from remembering,
but the harder I struggled, the more I was reminded.
It was no use making the effort.

We vowed not to say farewell.
I knew it was no use crying.

Though she left me,
her bright eyes, glowing cheeks and opulent lips
live in my heart.
Her sweet voice and dimpled smile
are with me too.

Memories of McDonalds, Starbucks, and
midnight movies are still with me.
The beaches of Waikiki we visited during summer vacation.
Central Park in autumn, trees ablaze with color.
Fallen leaves on the roadsides.
Blue sky over the snowy mountain.

The leaves are all off the trees and have traveled the globe.
Although our love may be buried
together with leaves,
her bright eyes, glowing cheeks and
opulent lips are still in my heart,
still alive in me.
Along with my fervent yearning.

At Abbotts Lagoon Beach

Here the reeds in the field are tossed about by winds.
Like an army of men in tasseled hats marching forward.

Swayed toward one side.
They do not behave themselves
against the winds.
They prefer to stand upright
to talk with heaven.
But winds pull them continuously
to go in their direction.

Sometimes when it is blowing a gale they weep loudly.
And when it rains they are filled with water.

The weather on this beach is frequently changing.
But always this salty breeze and humid air remains.
After suffering day and night, from winds in all directions
the heads of these reeds cannot help but hang down.

Calmly night falls here.
The whitish salt fields' panorama
spread out
beside the beach
flooded all over
with brilliant moonlight.

Fireflies in the Backyard

In the soft summer New Jersey night
fireflies in my backyard
flitting here and there
illuminating the blackness.

Each summer the fireflies return
reminding me of my childhood in Korea
in the rural community
where we were too poor to buy light.

Sometimes too poor to own a candle,
we collected fireflies in a basket
and read books by their sparks.

Fireflies delightedly giving off their radiance
brightening the dark garden.

A Heavy Silence

Between Powell Station and Aquatic Park
an old woman is dragged off a crowded Muni bus
—the Number 30—
by tall and sturdy policemen—one on each side.

With no money for a ticket
she is silent;
a lamb before slaughter,
a sheep before it is sheared.

With no money for proper clothing
she is dressed in rags.
Her thinning white hair
like the root of an onion.

She joins her hands together
in prayer and supplication.
Begs pardon with her tears.

She retreats
with a wagon filled with vegetables—parsnips and turnips.
A walking stick in her hand
insufficient to aid her.

The passengers on the bus
watch transfixed.
An old woman
bent with worry and fear,
and making little progress.

Thinking hard, no one says a word.
And the bus is filled with a heavy silence.

A Lucky Day

All through the morning, every day, an obscure saxophone player in New York
City wanders from place to place, setting up stage in Times Square, the Port
Authority Bus Terminal, Grand Central Station or the Empire State Building.

He places his worn-out hat (his only other possession) upturned, in front of his
feet.
With closed eyes he performs his favorite songs:
Oh Happy Day and *Gypsy's Nostalgia.*

Immersed in the playing he forgets his hunger, sorrow and loneliness.
When he plays the saxophone, it doesn't matter who listens.
But a lucky day is to hear loud applause from the audience.

Doorman

It is said that the first job the apartment doorman got
is the job he tried so hard to achieve for several years.

It is said he has never sat on a chair while working his shift
from six o'clock in the morning until ten o'clock at night,
arriving at the office before anyone else and leaving last.

It is said that he even eats lunch while standing up,
chewing his hamburger with one eye on the door,
eating hastily without any drink.

It is said by some people that when he uses the toilet
he must relieve himself in a few seconds,
he returns to his post so soon.

It is said he always smiles and greets the residents with a humble bow,
bowing down even to their dogs.

It is said he has never even applied for a leave
or taken a vacation.

It is said he has changed, become an old man too early, stooped with age;
that his face was altered,
that once he had a big smile.

But now he is like a mannequin
with only a resolute grin.

No Friend But a Stick

Among the people strolling in the park
a pedestrian walks with a stick.
Doing his best, moving little by little.

With each step he takes, the upper part of his body collapses.
His only friend, the stick, used like a cane, gives him the courage to stand up again.
And he struggles to his feet each time.

He continues this unnatural walking
diligently with absolute quiet.
As a pure white butterfly
follows behind.

While treading slowly, step-by-step, other people easily move ahead of him.
He stops and stares vacantly at the empty sky,
recalling nostalgic moments of bygone days
when he walked like others.

What is Seen

On my way home from work at the office
I stand reading a book in the aisle of the crowded subway,
Many more passengers are standing than sitting.

In a seat reserved for the disabled
a young couple watches a smartphone screen together
dressed alike in baseball caps and jean jackets

connected by a single set of headphones…
Arm in arm they are laughing together.
Almost one being.

Beside them, a snowy-haired grandmother stands
clutching the corner of the seat.
Limp and pale, she carries her burden—
a sack over her left shoulder.

At the next station a graceful and healthy woman gets on.
Seeing the young couple in the handicapped seat
she flashes her senior identification.

She sends them on their way.
Settling in with dignity.

The subway train continues to its final destination.
All of us will disembark soon.

Meteor Shower at Inwood Hill Park

In upper Manhattan one summer evening
I lie on the ground and look up at the sky;
Beyond the city lights, a myriad of stars and nebulae visible in the darkness.

Several meteors appear and disappear, like flickering lights.
While stationary stars like Polaris and the Big Dipper
hang on in the glittering sky.

Meteors' appear and disappear
in the twinkling of an eye.
I imagine that our life is also a flash in an eternity.

The Snail

After an evening of slight rain
a snail tries to move
in haste.

But slowly creeps
on the leaf
of a morning glory.

With tentacles for eyes
its pace
is slow,
intermittent
even…

This snail seems to think
before reaching its conclusion—
to move
from the old to the new.

North to south
forest floor to a peak of ocean
from fine to windy days.

Leaving a glimmer of itself,
marking a trail for others to follow.

A snail carries its universe
within a spiral shaped shell—
with all its thoughts and necessities.

Spending its effort all alone
preoccupied with moving to the next place only.
Solving its problems slowly.

The Patience of Heron

A white heron waits tranquilly for fish in a stream.
Not fussy about what size or type of fish
he waits.

Standing steady for an hour,
calmly, in an upright position.
So serene that even his breath seems to cease.

Slowly he bends his long neck.
The tasseled hairs on his head erect
as if imploring even the winds not to move.

He continues waiting until the fish come
then he shifts with lightning speed to catch it.

Biting the fish with his bill.
His mouth closed.
He waits while the fish writhes in agony.

He just keeps on waiting until the fish is completely exhausted.
Sometimes the fish is bigger than his head.
But he gradually swallows it wholly without chewing.

Squirrel

The squirrel is always so inquisitive about everything—
looking around restlessly while coming and going.

With his paws behind his ears he tries to hear the sounds
of the wind and the birdsong, even my breath.

Continually jumping up and down—changing his steps and the movement of his tail.
His body is lighter than air and softer than shadows.

Stealthy and furtive he walks quietly on the wind.
He moves shrewdly to transcend time and space.

Squirrel leisurely tilts his head and effortlessly walks the high-wire above.
Like a ping-pong ball he moves from branch to branch, tree to tree.

When he scurries down the aspen to look at me
he is burning with the same curiosity about me
as I feel for him.

For a little while the wind, birdsong, even breath
all seem to cease.
Even the second hand on the clock is still.

Deer

Without a sound she comes to my backyard
and like a shadow she disappears.
She is always silent.

She has no antlers, but two fawns.
Her quiet vigilance keeps them cozy,
as if they are still in the womb.

The mother's affection draws
the depth of the deep ocean
and her dark eyes hug them warmly.

She looks blankly at her shadow through the window
seeming to recollect her mate who has fled
leaving her with two little ones.

She has many things to mutter against him
but only chews over the good.
Ruminating the cud again and again.

Dolphin

You yearn to return home—
The way the night watchman waits for the morning.
But your dream is pathetic.

You are hungry and hanker for affection.
You stave off this famine with the anchovies
fed to you after you perform for the spectators.

In the aquarium you do flips, play ball and jump through hoops—
exercises you have practiced daily.
You really don't like entertaining,
but you do it to appease your desire.

You are my lovely friend.
A lover longing for the wide freedom of the ocean.
When will you return home?

Invisible Leash

At the training center a dog is tied to a stake—
a taut leash restrains him.

All day long he keeps trying to go further away
as if there were some chance of escape.

Sometimes he seems to forget his shackles.
And suddenly he rushes forward quickly.

But each time the leash tightens even more
and his body is jerked into the air.

Although he struggles with every fiber of his being
the distance he can move is not increased or decreased, and he seems diminished.

Today, the dog's trainer unties his leash.
At first the dog refuses to run forward—but leaps furiously in place.

Then, even after he goes out a sizable distance, he returns.
There is no leash now, but the distance between dog and stake is still taut.

Wandering Earthworms

On a summer morning, earthworms appear here and there
on the pathways where many people are coming and going.
The pedestrians do not mind the earthworms beneath their feet
keeping obsessively busy from sunup to late at night they haven't time to notice.

Earthworms might come out from their burrows to migrate or mate
not perceiving the serious danger they pose to pedestrians.
They might be searching for friends or families
wandering alone and roaming from place to place.

I imagine that someone could show them the best path to take…
Much as the creator looking at our lives might feel,
observing billions of humans who move around the world
without knowing death may be imminent in any given moment.

Imprisoned Words

Impatient and perplexed,
persistently scratching the floor with her claws.

Her large eyes
seem to speak
something urgent and painful.

But I have no ears to hear it.

All her requests to me, everything she wants,
seems to be in her eyes.
The words held back like tears that don't spill out.

Words that can find no way to come.

Even though she is making an appeal
still there is no sound; still the words
do not budge.

What I can do?
Only pass my hand over her head repeatedly.
Make a trip to a veterinarian.

Who can open the prison
that has confined these words
for millions of years?

You Are Mine

Every Wednesday Mrs. Brown frequents the grooming salon at PetSmart.
Though she makes an appointment, the salon is always busy.

She takes her poodle, Eddy for a haircut.
Sometimes a bath, blow dry and brush.
Nails manicured, polished, trimmed, all included in the price of the service.
For a healthy smile, she cleans Eddy's teeth at home every day.
Bathes Eddy with her shampoo, dries his body;
massages his coat with a mixture of jojoba oil, chamomile and aloe for a light finish.
She puts a pink ribbon in Eddy's hair, red shoes on his paws.

When she goes out she always puts shoes on the poodle—
in spite of Eddy's groans.
She puts a striped jacket on Eddy's back
even in sultry weather.
On sunny days she puts sunglasses on Eddy.
All his accessories are changed according to her desires, not Eddy's.

Mrs. Brown had a veterinarian cut Eddy's tail for a beauty show.
She almost had the vet cut off part of his ears!

She never thinks about Eddy's feelings at all.
She believes that Eddy belongs to her.
And doesn't think about the animate creature.

When a rainy day comes
Eddy turns round and round repeatedly.
Seeking a trace of his tail.

Hamlet Park Afternoon

Five-o-clock in the afternoon:
A village whose people love dogs.

Every afternoon big dogs out taking a walk with their people.
Sometimes the dogs and their masters just ahead of me…

Dogs let loose in a patch of grass.
Dogs move their bowels once free.

A Bulldog barks at a Greyhound for some reason.
A small mongrel wags its tail, sniffing another dog's anus.

A maiden embracing a poodle
enters the park.
Teenagers shouting to a Shepherd,
tossing a Frisbee to train him.

A middle-aged man in a blue beret
walks five dogs
past the children's playground.
The dragon tattoo on his forearm
bulging as he tries to restrain them.

A gray-haired couple
arrives at the entrance.
Disappointment and fear on their faces—
so many dogs!

A young woman pushes a baby carriage,
walking gingerly with her Boxer.

The sun sets behind the western mountains.
And the round full moon rises in the east.

Puberty

The weather is fine today
but yesterday was windy with rain.
The day before yesterday was also stormy.

Due to recent unexpected changes
it is not possible to forecast what the weather will be.

Today Emily didn't go to school;
and she didn't eat anything.
The day before yesterday she didn't go either,
but that was because of the rain.

Lately she received high scores in mathematics
but still was not happy. Sometimes she
convulses with laughter in her room or
whimpers without reason.

Sensitive to every little whisper
she responds with a scream.

Stifling his emotions, Emily's father firmly kicks
a rugby ball around the playground.
Uncertain where it will land.

A Living History of Sports and Entertainment

I'm going to dump my sports shoes in the trash.
Shoes which have been my faithful companions,
trainers and close friends for the last five years.

Though we didn't agree on much at first,
gradually we made concessions to each other.

Sometimes these shoes led me to the tennis court in the early morning
or took me to the playground for exercise.
I often trained hard in these shoes.

But on weekends and holidays they guided me to the perfect spot for a picnic
or to the mall for shopping.

When I fell ill they took me to the theater
to experience a living history of sports and entertainment.

Over time I felt these shoes
causing a strange imbalance in my body.

I discovered the bottom soles were worn irregularly.
Perhaps it was time for me to leave them.

It is regretful, but I had to abandon them.
Is there anything that does not grow old in this world?

Filing Cabinet

A rusty filing cabinet stands in the corner of my office.
The painting worn off, discolored.
The door is loosened, the doorknob twisted.
I have used it for more than twenty years,
even as a young businessman.

When she first came to my office
this model was new,
smart, and very smooth
each time I opened the door.
I was the only man to open her.

Nobody knew
the combination, but me.
I trusted the cabinet
with all kinds
of valuable documents.

Every day I opened and
closed it
repeatedly.

Sometimes I slept
in the office
all night with it.

I took my food and coffee
with the cabinet
nearby.

With my expanding business
other filing cabinets came into the office.

They were more colorful, fashionable
with modern functions and safety devices.

These new features—
so convenient and useful.

The battered cabinet became a place
merely for storing old documents.

Years later I forgot the combination.
I tried many times to open the drawers, to no avail.

It felt like rock. The door stayed firmly closed.
Until it was forced opened by a locksmith.

The Black Stone Mermaid: Is Life the Dream of Dreams?

There was a virgin, pure of heart, who was planning to marry a young man who worked on the newly formed crew of the RMS Titanic. The ship was on its maiden voyage, traveling from England to New York.

The port was clear as glass.
So smooth it was calm.
Truly that hour never had a sinister feeling
when he departed for New York.
The biggest ship ever built was cheered.
Merrily voyaged on her maiden journey.

Is life the dream of dreams?

But all dreams had vanished into the deep sea
as pieces of the ship crumbled.
Pieces of fantastic times.
Ecstatic days.

Yearning to lose herself in unattainable love
she didn't believe the news.
Couldn't believe in it.
Never admitted it.

"Fiancé never die, we are dreaming only.
The dream will be over very soon."

Is life the dream of dreams?

Though love has gone
memories remain.
Love stories don't fade.
She strongly held that
her fiancé would be coming back soon.
Of course.
Must be coming back. No doubt in her mind.
"Where is your vow? Give me back my heart. "

What is the yearning?
Is it a mist that appears for a little while
then just fades away?
Is it the dream of dreams for a moment?

From morning till evening.
Day to day.
Each month,
every year
of her life.

She sits at the beach
scans the horizon.
Waits for her fiancé.
Calls his name repeatedly.
No longer eats or sleeps.

Still there is no answer,
"Give me back my love, my heart!"

In silence and tears.
In silence and tears.
This yearning for unattainable love
burnt her heart.
The lovely body grew dark and blackened.

Sometime later she became a black stone.
Resembled a mermaid.
Left the world.

What is the yearning?
Is it a mist that appears for a little while
then vanishes like smoke?

Is life the dream of dreams?

Wasted Tire

In the corner of the sequestered village lies an abandoned tire.
Partially covered with once red, now blackened fallen leaves.
While the faint beams of sunset are lazing among the dropped leaves
the breeze blows in and more dried leaves descend.

An old man waiting for a bus looks at this scene for some time.
His forehead is lined with deep furrows
as he thinks dearly of the days gone by.

Now he runs with all his might toward the road ahead.
Like a slave who was kept well under the speed
in order not to be overtaken with the need to dash and scurry
like waves on the shore.

All his life he did his best, with these impediments.
But he couldn't keep the balance
of the time and tide.

That wasted tire might be thinking about speed it had known.
Remembering that speed is all of life.
Or it might be thinking for once in its life about resting awhile.

This day with its freedom from the snare,
it is comfortable with the leaves and breeze,
and its furrows are made smooth by the sunset's beams,
the way the old man's face is made serene with memories of long ago.

There Were Good Times Too

At the corner of New York City's Central Park,
Michael sets his fatigued body on some old newspapers,
with furrowed, unwashed face he looks down.

His comeliness gone.
His body bent and
drawn over ill-fitting attire.

Once, like others, he had a wife and home.
But now he has only a feeble body
and nightmares each evening.

To try and care for this weakened form he gets a meal sometimes.
He tries his best to survive in this strange land.
Making a livelihood to assimilate in this American society, but in vain.

After tasting life's sweetness,
now all is bitter.
Fallen into homelessness, this night he speaks.

"Hey, Michael, I am sorry.
You have always done well by me,
but what can I do?

You know well that sometimes there were good seasons.
Now I cannot do anything for you, not even offer a scrap of food
or any of those things you need.

I think I would rather go back to the homeland than suffer disgrace.
Then we may forsake hunger for freedom.
What do you think, my lovely body?"

Noise Control

A cargo truck ascends the steep rain-sopped road in heat-steamy weather.
The numbing noise of it hangs in the air
pushing on the trucks in front and behind it....

The truck is very slow and patched up looking—ugly.
But its speed is consistent.

Noise from the other trucks seem to add different colors
to its pushing power...
but in vain, the truck moves slowly still.

To escape the noisiness
some people block their ears or close their eyes.
Others leave quite quickly.

Under the shade of a tree—a free zone of quiet—
elders are discussing the luxury car
and appreciating the cicadas' singing.

The sweltering heat comes again and again more frequently,
and the truck's speed has not changed a bit.

Secluded Life

I live in a deep valley where there is no telephone,
no television, no computer.
No incoming news ... only the sounds
of sparrows and mountain streams.

I sit on a tree branch or a boulder,
dipping my feet in a stream,
and recall past days.
Yet surveying all I have toiled to achieve
everything seems meaningless.

Once I followed after rainbows,
chased after the wind.
I no longer struggle to exist, now.
I enjoy a life of seclusion
with nature as my neighbor.

When I miss my friends,
I go down to the post office and send a letter;
then return to my nest—
singing together with unidentified birds
and playing a game of hide-and-seek
with fawns in the forest.

Handwritten Letter

I wrote a handwritten letter to a dear old friend
who lives in the rural village of my homeland.

Over the past several years, I have sent only e-mails,
so now handwriting feels unfamiliar to me.

I place the letter in an envelope;
try to write his name and address on it.

At that moment, mountain brooks flow from my pen;
sparrows fly up and I hear the songs of the birds.

My study becomes the orchard hut; the farmland covered in green,
apricot pink blooms, plum blossoms, ripe cherries and apples.

In the heat of summer, the sound of thunder and bolts of lightning come;
In the fall, farmers store up grains in the barns for later.

Snowy winter comes,
then spring follows.
Even as the seasons change repeatedly,
our friendship is deepened.

I remove the letter from the envelope
and add a lyric he likes to the last line.

At the post office I quietly recall his name again,
and drop the letter into the mailbox.

My Father Is With Me

My father passed away a long time ago.
But he is still with me.
He never went to school.
But knew everything.
He knew what love was.

I loved my father like he loved me.
He was neither rich nor proud.
Never said to do good.
But did good works always.

My father knew the way to fix trust.
And keep it.
He knew the right way to sail through life's journey.

When I went astray in my life
he told me, "There is nothing you cannot do."

My father was not a doctor,
but he healed the sickness of my body and mind.
When I grew weak,
he trained and disciplined me.

My father has passed away.
But he is in my heart as a master compass.
My soul is always steeped in joy with him.
In his breast I sleep,
dreaming in the sound
his breathing kept,
and in the surging crowd,
toiling, striving from day to day.

Knowing whatever happens,
my father is with me.

The Train Passes

The train passes along the Hudson River,
Its whistle heard all along the riverside.
If there were no whistles in this city, how prosaic life would be.

Every time the train goes by, the river's waves lick about the ships,
drowsy flowers beside the bank awaken from their midday nap,
and people turn to brooding and imagining the places they might be carried.

The train is bringing the passengers and their dreams
together with my empty mind;
passing by the river bank, the open field and across the country.

The train is puffing away along the railroad, where the green signal lamp
beckons.
The train passes by the autumn forest and the dark shadows pass over.
My mind follows them aimlessly.

While Changing the Calendar

While I exchange last year's calendar for a new one
days flit through my mind like moving pictures.

Many days have vanished; where are they?
When did they leave me?

It isn't easy to remember the days,
even though I think back or look deeply into history.

Now I turn the faded calendar
and memories return.

The days jumping over other days,
just as I fold the months back again.

On a certain day, some people throw a stone,
some cast a net, and some sing a song.
Now all of them have gone.

While opening this year's calendar I tell myself:
"An old year has gone and a new one has come.
I begin again toward my happy dream."

Han-Jae Lee has studied poetry at Chung-Ang University and Korea University, and in the United States at library workshops in Santa Cruz, San Jose and at the Hudson Valley Writers' Center in New York. In 2005 his poem, "A High-rise Apartment," won a silver award in a national contest sponsored by The National Assembly of Korea and The Federation of Korean Cultural Center. His first poetry collection, *A High-rise Apartment*, was published in Korea in 2008. He also co-published three poetry anthologies, and his poems have appeared in several Korean literary magazines. His debut collection in English, *The Golden Gate Bridge and Other Natural Wonders*, was published by River Sanctuary Publishing in 2013. His chapbook, *A Place Where Clouds Are Flowing*, was published by Finishing Line Press in 2017. Lee's poems have appeared in *Catamaran Literary Reader, Monterey Poetry Review, Caesura, Sand Hill Review, Crab Orchard Review, PCC Inscape Magazine, Military Experience & The Arts,* and *EMRYS Journal.*